A Trail
of
Memories

Also available in Large Print
by Louis L'Amour:

The First Fast Draw
The Haunted Mesa
Passin' Through
Dutchman's Flat
Night Over the Solomons
The Rider of the Ruby Hills
Riding for the Brand
The Trail to Crazy Man
Jubal Sackett

A Trail of Memories

Memories

The Quotations of Louis L'Amour

Compiled by
Angelique L'Amour

Foreword by Louis L'Amour

"Pa, he used to say that no memory is ever alone, it's at the end of a trail of memories, a dozen trails that each have their own associations."

Ride the River

G.K.HALL & CO.
Boston, Massachusetts
1989

Published in Large Print by arrangement with
Bantam Books, a division of Bantam Doubleday Dell
Publishing Group, Inc.

G.K. Hall Large Print Book Series.

Set in 18 pt Plantin.

Library of Congress Cataloging in Publication Data

L'Amour, Louis, 1908-
  A trail of memories : the quotations of Louis L'Amour / compiled by
  Angelique L'Amour : foreword by Louis L'Amour.
    p.   cm. — (G.K. Hall large print books series)
    ISBN 0-8161-4728-0 (lg. print)
    1. L'Amour, Louis, 1908- —Quotations. 2. Large type books.
I. L'Amour, Angelique.   II. Title.
[PS3523.A446A6   1989]
813'.52—dc19   88-39881

To my father—
  Forever my inspiration,
  and the first man in my life.
  I love you, Dad.

Contents

Acknowledgments

This book would not have been possible without the guidance, support, and friendship of three very special people . . . I extend my warmest thanks to Stuart Applebaum, Barbara Alpert, and Barb Burg.

—Angelique L'Amour

Foreword

by Louis L'Amour

Characters have a way of taking on a life on their own, expressing themselves in the simple philosophy of their times, and expressing beliefs acquired through living, working, and being. Once characters are established, they become their own persons and the ideas of the characters are such ideas as they might have acquired in the circumstances of their daily existence. Yet, I suppose it is virtually impossible to entirely free the character from the creator, so I cannot disclaim responsibility for the quotations that follow.

When I write, the story takes over, and when first I read or heard quotations from my work, I recognized none of them, isolated as they were. They were created in the natural course of writing, without forethought or planning, and in many cases are better understood as a part of a story's progression and of character development.

My daughter, Angelique, compiled this

collection, and the idea of doing so was hers. Here and there I might have wished to leave out a few quotations but she said no, and our publisher agreed with her. A lot of reading and hard work was involved, and I believe that in a few cases she read books of mine for the first time. In the process of her finishing school and becoming an actress, there was never enough time for her to do much outside reading.

So we must share together the responsibility for what follows: I for writing these words, and she for gathering them together for those interested readers.

Introduction

by Angelique L'Amour

> "You've heard him talk. He's got a way
> about him, a way with words. He can
> make the temple bells tinkle for you, and
> you can just hear them big old elephants
> shuff-shuffling along, the priests callin'
> folks to prayer and the like."
>
> *The Lonesome Gods*

Every morning from the time I was a little
girl until I left for college I would sit down
at the breakfast table with my father, my
mother, and my older brother Beau, and
Dad would read to us. It was a wonderful
time of day. The books he read to us were
generally ones he needed to read for his research, but there were others—biographies
and histories and the H.M.S. *Hornblower* na-
val adventure series. There were also the
times he read his own books to us. This
didn't happen too often, maybe six or seven
times as I grew up. There was magic when

he read his own words, for I believe he writes to be read aloud. Not many authors write prose so poetic that it is as easy to listen to as it is to read.

Because of this daily breakfast ritual, and my mother reading children's books to me at night ("I read you the fun stuff," she always said), I developed a love of books and reading, of language and learning. This is perhaps the single most important lesson I learned from my parents.

When I was very young Dad explained to me that he had a time machine in his office. Through books, he said, I could go anywhere at any time and be anyone at all without leaving the room. That is the magic of reading. It inspires the imagination. That is what he does in his books: He creates a time and a place and transports the reader there. His office is lined wall to wall and floor to ceiling with books—all of them opportunities to learn and experience life through words.

I remember as a little girl going into his office. He'd sit me down in his big black chair and tell me stories. Sometimes we'd both be characters in them, having some marvelous adventure together. Perhaps that is where my love for acting came from: playing a character in one of these stories. Listening to his exciting tales led me to see my father as quite a hero. Later, as I got older, I would hear stories about his own growing up, and I realized that in his own way my father was an adventurer as well as a hero. That is one of the reasons the fights in his books seem so real. I get the feeling Dad actually delivered and received those punches. Recently, he told me about times during his yondering days when he was walking through the mountains in Tibet. The trail had narrowed to three inches wide, with a couple-hundred-foot drop on one side, and he'd wondered just what in the world he was doing there. His early life seemed to us a series of adventures, not all of them fun. But Dad has said many times, "Adventure is just a romantic name for trouble."

In part, I learned to read by watching and listening to my father. Starting from the time I could get out of a chair by myself, I would stand behind him and read over his shoulder. He would show me where he was on the page and I would follow along as he read aloud. Soon I started to read by myself.

When I first began to read my father's books I read for pure enjoyment. Later, I finally understood what some of his fan mail had meant. Women who were raising children without husbands had written to him that they were raising their children on the teachings in his books. They'd told their sons that if they grew up to have the morals and values of his characters, they would be good men. Men to be proud of, men to shape the world.

Many of the things my father's characters think are important to growing and learning are the beliefs Dad has tried to instill in both my brother and me. These ideas started jumping off the page at me as I read. Finally, I went to my father and read a few to him, and he told me about something that had happened to him a little while earlier. He had been invited as one of three writers to speak at a teachers' conference. The moderator began introducing the first speaker by reading some quotes from one of the author's books. The ideas expressed were intelligent and primarily about learning. Dad waited to find out who had written them and was surprised when he was introduced as the author of those words. He hadn't remembered writing them, and until that point, hadn't quite realized the magnitude of the lessons taught to his readers.

The quotations that follow are ones that

have affected me and my life. They focus on things that my father stressed as important as I was growing up. They cover a broad range of topics, from learning and loving to self-defense and survival in the wilderness. My father made sure that my brother and I learned about survival at an early age, because we were always way out in the middle of nowhere on school vacations traveling with Dad while he did research for his books.

Many of my father's readers have expressed an interest in his autobiography. But by reading his words, each reader has met a part of my father. Each hero has a bit of Dad's experience that makes him who he is. With Lando it was all those boxing matches as Dad grew up. With Barnabas Sackett it is the sailor and explorer in my father. Each of his heroines has a bit of my mother in her. The romances in each story express love the way my father sees it, and sometimes love the way it is between my parents.

My father is a poet, so for that reason I chose some of the quotes for the sheer beauty of the words. Others I chose for what they teach us. My father always said that age is unimportant and that we should always listen to people and what they have to say because education is everywhere. The most important thing—along with love of learning and reading, he says—is always to head somewhere in your life, do something. You may decide to change direction, but at least you are being creative.

I think that this collection of quotations from my father's books reveals much of what makes Dad who he is—in a very different way than his autobiography will—for these words are the heart and soul of what he believes and what he wants to leave behind—not only to Beau and myself, but to all his readers.

A Trail
of
Memories

Life

If man is to vanish from the earth, let him vanish in the moment of creation, when he is creating something new, opening a path to the tomorrow he may never see. It is man's nature to reach out, to grasp for the tangible on the way to the intangible.

The Lonesome Gods

To challenge the fates, that is living! To ride the storm, to live daringly, to live nobly, not wasting one's life in foolish, silly risks, or ruining the brain with too much wine, or with hashish!

The Walking Drum

Living a life is much like climbing mountains—the summits are always further off than you think, but when a man has a goal, he always feels he's working toward something.

The Lonely Men

1

A man living off the country and in a land where there's risk at every hand does not get much time to contemplate himself. . . . Each day is a day to live and in which to keep from dying, and a man's energies are directed out from himself and his thoughts as well. Contemplation is a leisure indulgence. It is for a man in an armchair or beside a fire in his own house. It isn't for a man whose every sense is attuned to sounds outside himself.

Jubal Sackett

What is it that has made me happy? A deck beneath my feet, a horse between my knees, a sword in my hand, or a girl in my arms! These I have loved, and the horizon yonder, beyond which there is the unknown.

The Walking Drum

Life teaches us much of which we are not aware. Our senses perceive things that do not impinge upon our awareness, but they lie dormant within us and affect our recognition of people and conditions.

The Walking Drum

One can waste half a lifetime with people one doesn't really like or doing things when one would be better off somewhere else.

Ride the River

All life is based on decisions. Decide now on what you'd like to become and what you would like to do. The two are not necessarily the same, although sometimes they can be.

The Lonesome Gods

To live is not only to exist. It is not to wait for supper of an evening or for bedtime or for a drink at a saloon. It is all of these things and every marvelous moment that comes between. To live is to feel, and the senses have more to teach than the mind. More, at least, for the immediate moment. It is better, sometimes, to simply *feel*, to simply *be*.

Bendigo Shafter

No man is lost while yet he lives.

The Walking Drum

Up to a point a man's life is shaped by environment, heredity, and movements and

3

changes in the world about him; then there comes a time when it lies within his grasp to shape the clay of his life into the sort of thing he wishes to be. . . . Everyone has it within his power to say, this I am today, that I shall be tomorrow.

The Walking Drum

A man's life is a precious thing, though he waste it. A life is greater than gold and better than all else, so who am I to take it unless need be?

The Warrior's Path

He rode because he was Jeremy Ring, a gallant follower of lost or flimsy causes, a poet with a sword, a man for whom life was a thing to be nobly used, not allowed to rust or wither and decay.

Sackett's Land

. . . and if I have not written words upon paper as I should like to have done, I have written large upon the page of life that was left open for me.

The Lonely Men

4

May your shadow never grow less.
The Walking Drum

I like a confident man. . . . Especially if he lives.

Sackett's Land

This—this was what made life: a moment of quiet, the water falling in the fountain, the girl's voice . . . a moment of captured beauty. He who is truly wise will never permit such moments to escape.

The Walking Drum

Pa, he always taught us boys to make up our minds, and once made up, to act on what we decided, and not waste time quibbling.

Mojave Crossing

It seems to me that blue blood only becomes important when red blood begins to run thin.

The Walking Drum

. . . neither of us is going to get out of this alive. That's the only thing a man knows about life.

Conagher

Opportunity

He put his hand upon my shoulder and told me that in the world were two kinds of people, those who wish and those who will, and the world and its goods will always belong to those who will.

The Warrior's Path

Now, a body never knows when he starts out to do something just what will come of it, else maybe nothing would ever get done.

Chancy

I had found no luck and no opportunity except that I made.

Sackett's Land

Need and desire have no connection. . . . Many people desire things they do not need.

7

Happiness can be measured by what one does not need, but often to see is to want.

Jubal Sackett

When one has lost his freedom it is always a long walk back.

The Walking Drum

. . . any man can be a slave, and a few men, if they will it, can become kings.

The Warrior's Path

Are we not all slaves, occasionally? To custom? To a situation? To an idea? Who among us is truly free?

The Walking Drum

The United States is our country, too, and if we do not make the most of it, the fault is ours.

Last of the Breed

I want him to understand what is happening here, then go on to something bigger, better. Happiness for a man usually means doing

8

something he wants to do very much, something that gives him a sense of achievement.

Bendigo Shafter

Trade is much superior to piracy. You can rob and kill a man but once, but you can cheat him again and again.

The Walking Drum

Pa, he always said a man had to look spry for himself, because nobody would do it for him; your opportunities didn't come knocking around, you had to hunt them down and hog-tie them.

Chancy

Nobody got anywhere in this world by simply being content.

Bendigo Shafter

Hard Work

A man should build. He should always build.
Sackett's Land

. . . [I] looked up in darkness at the hand-hewn rafters. A knowing hand had shaped them, a knowing hammer drove the pegs. There is a quiet beauty in such things as these, a beauty more than paint or chisel make, the beauty of quiet men, making strong things for their own use, shaping each piece with loving fingers.
To the Far Blue Mountains

Wherever a man is, there is work to do.
Bendigo Shafter

It was a rough, hard, wonderful life and it took men with the bark on to live it. We didn't ask anything of anybody and as long as a man did his work nobody cared what else he was or did.

Galloway

The white man respects success. For the poor, the weak, and the inefficient, he has pity or contempt. Whatever the color of your skin, whatever country you come from, he will respect you if you do well what it is you do.

Treasure Mountain

A cowhand is a damned fool who will work twenty-five hours out of every day if he can do it from a saddle. But put him on his feet, and you've got yourself a man who is likely to sit down and build himself a smoke so's he can think about it. And after he thinks it over, he'll get back in the saddle and ride off.

The Sackett Brand

What a man wants to do he generally can do, if he wants to badly enough.

Bendigo Shafter

Own a few acres, lad, and keep it unen-

cumbered and you'll not want for some'at to eat. You can always grow a few cabbages.
Sackett's Land

. . . there's work a man can do that's helpful to his thinking, and working with the hands is one way.
Bendigo Shafter

You don't build a country like this on sweat alone, ma'am.
Lonely on the Mountain

They are the men who will make this town into a city. They have ideas, but they do not merely have ideas, they put the ideas to work.
The Lonesome Gods

The world isn't built around people who do what they want to do . . . what they want regardless of who gets hurt. It is built by people who do what they *should* do.
Bendigo Shafter

Statesmanship is about ten percent good ideas and motives and ninety percent getting backing for your program.

Every man to his job, mine's politics. First thing is to listen. Learn the issues, the personalities, where the votes are, where the hard feelings are.

The Daybreakers

History is best made by men with hands. Brains are well enough, but count for nothing without the hands to build, to bring to fulfillment.

Sackett's Land

Our struggle was for time. Our leisure was bought from hardship, and we needed leisure to think, to dream, to create.

Bendigo Shafter

My friend, there is a Hell. It's when a man has a family to support, has his health, and is ready to work, and there is no work to do. When he stands with empty hands and sees his children going hungry, his wife without the things to do with. I hope you never have to try it.

Bendigo Shafter

. . . it is the work a man does that matters. Many men who have made mistakes in their own lives have created grandly, beautifully. It is this by which we measure a man, by what he does in this life, by what he creates to leave behind.

Bendigo Shafter

Family and Home

If you step on one Sackett's toes, they all come running.

Ride the River

A name is what a man makes it. . . . My father did well with his and I hope to do as much. The times are changing, and many people are restless with the desire to better themselves. We have too many gentlemen who do nothing, are nothing, and many a yeoman or apprentice with ability who would rise in position if the chance existed. . . . Here there is no such restriction. . . . Then the secret is to come first and help to make the rules by which the rest will live.

Sackett's Land

One chooses a name if one wills, perhaps one more suited to the personality. After all, only a few inherit great names. The rest must make them for ourselves. . . .

The Warrior's Path

It sounded like a made-up name, but I'd known folks with real names that sounded made up.

Mojave Crossing

Nobody ever did ask him his name, as folks just didn't ask questions. Whatever somebody named you or whatever you answered to was good enough.

Lonely on the Mountain

A man's name is his own.

The Walking Drum

. . . I learned a long time ago that a name is only what a person makes it.

Lonely on the Mountain

Besides, what does a name mean? Nothing, until a man makes it mean something.

Passin' Through

16

To be born of an eminent family is nothing if you are nothing yourself.

Sackett's Land

. . . he was also a Sackett, and blood runs thicker than branch water.

Mojave Crossing

But I am somebody . . . I am *me*. I like being me, and I need nobody to make me somebody. I need no setting. As for a home, I can build my own. As for position, each of us finds his own.

Comstock Lode

. . . some of the great families of the world were founded with nothing but a sword and a strong right arm.

Sackett's Land

It is said that there were some respected men among my ancestors, too, but my father paid little attention to that. He judged each man by himself and not by his ancestors.

Jubal Sackett

What a man is and what he becomes is in part due to his heritage. . . .

Sackett's Land

My father often said that he knew of no king with a family half as old as his own. Not that the age of the family was important, many an old tree bears bad fruit.

The Walking Drum

"Only way we can help Archie . . . is to stay alive. If he isn't dead already, they will try to keep him alive and sell him. We'll find him then and see he's freed, if I have to bring all the Sacketts down from the hills."

"How many are there? Of the Sacketts, I mean?"

"Nobody rightly knows, but even one Sackett is quite a few."

Ride the River

No matter that it made little sense to some . . . a man must have something in which to believe, and with us who were Tennessee Sacketts the family came first.

The Sackett Brand

He had been the best of fathers and it was never easy to be a father to strong sons growing up in a strange land, each coming to manhood, each asserting himself, loving the father yet wishing to be free of him, finding fault to make the break easier. So it had been since the world began, for the young do not remain young and the time must come when each must go out on his own grass.

Jubal Sackett

"My friend," he said, "I do not know what else I shall leave my son, but if I have left him a love of language, of literature, a taste for Homer, for the poets, the people who have told our story—and by 'our' I mean the story of mankind—then he will have legacy enough."

The Lonesome Gods

That was how I would remember my father. There was never a place he walked that was not the better for his having passed. For every tree he cut down he planted two.

Jubal Sackett

. . . most of all I wished my mother to sit for a while in the sunset of her life, just to sit and live the sounds of our hills, the light and shadows upon them.

Ride the River

A boy should know his pa—he needs somebody to look up to. A boy or a girl, they learn how to be a man or a woman by watching their folks.

Conagher

Odd thing, I'd never thought of my pa as a person. I expect a child rarely does think of his parents that way. They are a father and a mother, but a body rarely thinks of them as having hopes, dreams, ambitions and desires and loves. . . . I got to wondering if he ever doubted himself like I did, if he ever felt short of what he wished to be, if he ever longed for things beyond him that he couldn't quite put into words.

Lando

Men without fathers often place more emphasis on them than others would. A mill does not turn on water that is past.

The Walking Drum

A wife and family don't go along with dreams. They hamper a man's movements, they restrict the risks he can afford to take to get ahead, and even the most helpful of women is usually more expense than a very young man can bear.

Bendigo Shafter

Riches are a claim to distinction for those who have no other right to it. Ancestry is most important to those who have done nothing themselves, and often the ancestor from whom they claim descent is one they would not allow in the house if they met him today.

The Walking Drum

Treat the earth kindly, my friends, and it will give you comfort, security, and all a man may need. If you plant a flake of gold in the earth, will anything come of it? But plant a seed and it will repay you many times over.

Comstock Lode

Folks had it down that I was a wanderin' man, but most wanderin' men I've known only wandered because of the home they expected to find . . . *hoped* to find, I mean.

Treasure Mountain

Pa told us we held the land in trust. We were free to use it so long as it was kept in shape for the generations following after, for our sons and yours.

Ride the Dark Trail

A strong son makes a father proud.

The Walking Drum

They had been warm shelters, and when does a man leave a place he has lived without some regret? For each time some part of him is left behind.

Jubal Sackett

It is a danger . . . to live always in one city, for undue emphasis is placed upon the importance of those who live there. Often when compared to others, their shadows grow less.

The Walking Drum

It seems to me that first a man tries to get shelter and food to eat, but as soon as he has that he tries to find beauty, something to warm the heart and the mind, something to ease the thoughts and make pleasurable the sitting in the evening.

Galloway

To build a house is one thing, but to make it a home is quite another. . . .

Bendigo Shafter

I wanted a place they could grow up with, where they could put down roots. I wanted a place they'd be proud to come back to and which they could always call home . . . no matter how far they went or what happened.

The Daybreakers

A man that old should have himself a home, a place to hang his hat while he waited for the sunset.

Conagher

We had come a far piece into a strange land, a trail lit by lonely camp fires and by gun-fire, and the wishing we did by day and by night. Now we rode back to plant roots in the land, and with luck, to leave sons to carry on a more peaceful life, in what we hoped would be a more peaceful world.

The Sky-Liners

Women

. . . it runs in the blood of a man that he should care for womenfolk. It's a need in him, deep as motherhood to a woman, and it's a thing folks are likely to forget. . . . If he's to feel of any purpose to himself, he's got to feel he's needed, feel he stands between somebody and any trouble.

The Sky-Liners

I always said . . . that I wanted a woman to walk beside me, not behind me.

Sackett's Land

There are men who prefer to keep trouble from a woman, but it seems to me that is neither reasonable nor wise. I've always respected the thinking of women, and also their ability to face up to trouble when it comes,

25

and it shouldn't be allowed to come on them unexpected.

Mojave Crossing

She'll stand to it. There's a likely craft, lad, and one to sail any sea. You can see it in the clear eyes of her and the way she carries her head. Give me always a woman with pride, and pride of being a woman. She's such a one.

The Warrior's Path

Most of my years I'd spent shying around in the mountains or out on the prairie lands, with no chance to deal myself any high cards in society, but believe me, there's more snares in a woman's long lashes than in all the creek bottoms of Tennessee.

Mojave Crossing

Have a son by all means, but choose the lady well. Breeding counts for much in dogs, horses, and men. Breed for strength, health, and stamina, but for wisdom, too. . . . You will see many women, and often you will think yourself in love, but temper passion with wisdom, my son, for sometimes the glands speak louder than the brain. Each man owes a debt to his family, his country and his species to leave sons and daughters who will lead, inspire, and create.

Sackett's Land

Anyway, womenfolks have to find a man with roots, a man who belongs somewhere or to something. She's got to take into account she may have a child and she's got to have a roof over her head and a place to raise him. A woman's generally lookin' for a man with cattle on the hills or goods on the shelf, and well she should be.

Passin' Through

A woman needs a man, Bendigo, even a woman like Ruth Macken. No woman, however strong, should have to stand alone. Believe me, she's a stronger woman because Cain is there and she knows he's there.

Bendigo Shafter

Man's greatest advantage in the battle of the sexes is woman's curiosity.

The Walking Drum

. . . it has occurred to me that a man need know but two sentences to survive. The first to ask for food, the second to tell a woman he loves her. If he must dispense with one or the other, by all means let it be the first. For surely, if you tell a woman you love her, she will feed you.

The Walking Drum

You assume such a girl would have less courage than you? Less fortitude? You do not understand my sex, Barnabas.

Sackett's Land

A man who has not known many women cannot appreciate the value of one.

The Walking Drum

Look out for the women. You never know whether they're going to scream, or faint, or go for a gun.

Mustang Man

When a talking woman sits quiet a man had better look at his hole card and keep a horse saddled.

Ride the Dark Trail

"Ma'am," I said, "you're a lot of woman on the outside." She stiffened up like I'd slapped her. "What do you mean by that?"

"Well, I sure don't cut no figure as a man knowing women, but it seems to me what you wear is a lot of feeling where it shows. I don't think there's very much down inside. . . . I'd as soon make love to you, ma'am, but I'd want to keep both your hands in sight. I'd never know which one held the knife."

Mojave Crossing

. . . but I was wakeful as a man with three sparkin'-age daughters.

Lonely on the Mountain

When one is young, one does not think of gold but only of the light in a maiden's eyes.

The Walking Drum

. . . pretty women sometimes can do things no man would attempt.

The Lonesome Gods

29

. . . she is not to dream about, my friend, she *is* the dream.

Sackett's Land

My shadow is small before the sun of your beauty.

The Walking Drum

. . . you were in love with what you thought she was. A man often creates an image of a girl in his mind but when it comes right down to it that's the only place the girl exists.

The Daybreakers

What of Itchakomi? Such a woman walks with the wind. Such a woman must be fought for or stolen.

Jubal Sackett

[He was] . . . frightened himself but braver because he was needed, because she needed him. Her need had made him stronger, helped to bring him through what followed.

Comstock Lode

30

"Trouble is, no woman in her right mind would marry a fool, and I'm certainly one."

"A lot you know about women!" she scoffed. "Did you ever see a fool who didn't have a wife?"

Come to that, I hadn't.

Sackett

A woman can always find something in a man worth having.

Conagher

A true gentleman is at a disadvantage in dealing with women. Women are realists, and their tactics are realistic, so no man should be a gentleman where women are concerned unless the women are very, very old or very, very young. Women admire gentlemen, and sleep with cads.

The Walking Drum

Many a man who had no thought of marrying suddenly finds himself in a place when he's either got to marry or run.

Bendigo Shafter

Law and order were made for women. They

31

are hedged around by protection. But out in the wilderness they are only as safe as men will let them be.

Mustang Man

But she was a woman, with a woman's love to give, and she needed someone reaching out for it. There was an emptiness within her, a yearning that must be fulfilled, a love that needed to be given.

Conagher

. . . for I am one that from his earliest days has loved the physical delights: the warmth of the sun, the drinking of cold, clear water, the taste of salt spray, the damp feel of fog upon the flesh, and the touch of a woman's hands.

The Walking Drum

. . . I had observed that masculine beauty as an enticer of the female is much overrated. Women are led to the boudoir by the ears. For one who talks well, with a little but not too much wit, it is no problem.

The Walking Drum

Had she known my mind she would have been unworried, for there was no wealth anywhere that meant half so much as a glance from her eyes or the shape of her body beneath her thin clothing.

The Walking Drum

When a woman sees a man she wants, there's no need to promise or even say very much. A woman will come up with better answers than any poor mountain boy could think up.

Ride the River

We had met as equals, rarely a good thing in such matters, for the woman who wishes to be the equal of a man usually turns out to be less than a man and less than a woman. A woman is herself, which is something altogether different than a man.

The Walking Drum

Gals like the high-spirited, high-headed kind, I've noticed. If they can break them to harnass they aren't at all what the gal wanted in the beginning, and if she can't break them they usually break her. But's that the way of it.

Galloway

You've got to admit she's pretty much of a woman, and she was always the lady. But you've got to admit she keeps what she's got so you know it's there.

Mojave Crossing

But she was a fair lady, a girl's bright eyes have won the day more than once, and I was the fool ever to look into them. For I am an unhandsome man, and the romance in my heart does not show past the bend in my nose, or at least the girls don't seem to look beyond that.

Mustang Man

How long is a girl a child? She is a child, and then one morning you wake up and

she's a woman and a dozen different people
of whom you recognize none.

Bendigo Shafter

A man you can figure on; a woman you
can't. They're likely either to faint, or to
grab for a gun regardless of consequences.

Chancy

A woman who has trapped her game has a
different way about her than one who is still
on the stalk.

The Warrior's Path

Mostly a man just thinks about women, and
they all get to look mighty fine after a while.
A body forgets how mean and contrary they
can be, and he just thinks of them as if they
were angels or something.

The Sky-Liners

She looks like a passionate woman, but she

isn't, son. Take it from me, the great courtesans of the past . . . were never passionate, loving women. They were cold, calculating. They used the emotions of men for their own purposes, they were all show, all promises.

Mojave Crossing

Women? Ah, women were the stuff of dreams, made to be loved, and he who could say the reality was less than the promise was neither lover nor dreamer.

The Walking Drum

We will talk of wars and women, the worries of one, the wiles of the other.

Sackett's Land

The deep sea can be fathomed, but who knows the heart of a woman?

The Walking Drum

Now, I was never one to lie or to make light of trouble with womenfolks. There's men

36

who feel they should, but I've found women stand well in trouble, and there's no use trying to make it seem less than it is. They won't believe you, anyway.

The Sky-Liners

Women are neither weaklings nor fools, and they, too, must plan for what is to come. He who does not prepare his woman for disaster is a fool.

The Walking Drum

Most men do not give a woman credit for intelligence. . . . And that may be an advantage.

The Lonesome Gods

All women are strange until they become familiar, but I have forgotten other women. How could even a memory be left after having seen you?

The Walking Drum

37

Not too complete—to be too complete is often to be lonely. A man needs a woman and a woman a man. It is the way of things.

The Lonesome Gods

"It may give her time to discover herself, to find out who she is."

"You're talking nonsense, Shafter, and you know it. Nobody is anybody until they make themselves somebody."

Bendigo Shafter

And as for women? . . . For the moment I loved them, and for the moment, no doubt, they loved me, and who can say how long such moments can last? I drink the wine and put aside the glass, but the taste lingers . . . the taste lingers.

The Walking Drum

Any time is a time for thinking of women . . . and when they thrust the blade that takes my life I shall be thinking of women, or of a woman. If not, then death has come too late.

The Walking Drum

Love, Friendship, and Loyalty

Love is a moment of stillness that sometimes a word can shatter to fragments, or love can be a thing that endures, a rich deep current that flows unending down the years.

The Walking Drum

Sometimes the most important things in a man's life are the ones he talks about least.

The Daybreakers

I said he did not need anyone. I did not say that he did not want someone. He told me once that happiness was born a twin, that it must be shared.

The Lonesome Gods

What can the will do when the heart commands?

The Walking Drum

"When you wish to go to the mountains," she said, "you may go, and if you wish it, I will go with you, and when you make your camp, I will cook your meat, and when you wish to sleep, I will prepare your bed. Where you go, I will go."

Jubal Sackett

Who is to say? What is love? Perhaps for a time I loved her; perhaps in a way I love her still. Perhaps when a man has held a woman in his arms, there is a little of her with him forever.

The Walking Drum

You don't understand. I like the theater. It is exciting and interesting to me. If I leave, it will only be for love, and because I am very sure that I have found the right man. Whether he is wealthy or not would never be a consideration, just that he's someone with whom I could be happy, someone I could respect.

Comstock Lode

Who is not a fool? Often when one is in love one can only win by losing.

The Walking Drum

41

I do not even know what love is. I only know that I felt good when near him, lost when he went from me.

Last of the Breed

People often fall in love with those who resemble them because they can imagine no beauty greater than their own.

The Walking Drum

To keep a friend is important and to shame him would be to lose him.

Jubal Sackett

A man's success he can share with others, his troubles are his own.

Comstock Lode

I'm a visitor here . . . and a man has no call to get blood on a neighbor's carpet.

Lonely on the Mountain

Wust thing a man can do is whup a Sackett. They'll dog you to your dyin' day.

Lonely on the Mountain

. . . we had shared violence and struggle and it is a deep tie.

The Daybreakers

He'll do to ride the river with.

Chancy

. . . I've covered a lot of country in my time, but when I take a man's money I ride for the brand.

Conagher

. . .trail dust is thicker'n blood. . . .

The Daybreakers

Time

There will come a time when you believe everything is finished. That will be the beginning.

Lonely on the Mountain

. . . to let myself waste time in worrying—time that I'd best spend doing something. One thing I'd learned over the years: never to waste time moaning about what couldn't be helped. If a body can do something, fine—he should do it. If he can't, then there's no use fussing about it until he *can* do something.

The Sackett Brand

For you and me, today is all we have; tomorrow is a mirage that may never become reality.

The Walking Drum

44

Few of us ever live in the present, we are forever anticipating what is to come or remembering what has gone. . . .

Bendigo Shafter

Seems to me a man can most usually take time to contemplate, and if he does it will save him a lot of riding and a lot of headaches.

The Sky-Liners

A year? What is a year? All time is relative. One day may be a lifetime, a year can be forever. It is not the number of days but what goes into those days.

The Warrior's Path

A mill grinds no corn with water that is past.

Lando

Twenty years? It is a long time. A man remembers a woman, a fight, perhaps a very good horse for twenty years, but not much else.

Treasure Mountain

Men always had reason to measure time, for ceremonies and the like, but sometimes I think we'd all be better off if we had no clocks or calendars. Then we might never get old, for we wouldn't know the passing of time.

Bendigo Shafter

I do not think much of ages. People are people. What does it matter how old or young they are? It is a category, and I do not like categories.

The Lonesome Gods

Ours is too busy a world, and there is no time for considering.

The Warrior's Path

No man should go down the long way without leaving something behind him, and all I've got to leave will disappear when the dust settles.

Treasure Mountain

Growth and Change

. . . growth comes from change. A people grows or it dies.

Jubal Sackett

The one law that does not change is that everything changes, and the hardship I was bearing today was only a breath away from the pleasures I would have tomorrow, and those pleasures would be all the richer because of the memories of this I was enduring.

Galloway

Circumstances can change in a mighty short time where the country is growing, and the West they had heard about was, for the most of it, already gone.

The Sky-Liners

We grow wise, you and I, but in wisdom there is often pain. No man of my people has traveled so far. None but me has crossed the great water, none but me has seen the great cities and the horses and carriages. But if they will not believe what I have seen, if I am no longer great among my people—then I am an empty man, Sack-ett.

To the Far Blue Mountains

I would not sit waiting for some vague to-morrow, nor for something to *happen*. One could wait a lifetime, and find nothing at the end of the waiting. I would begin here, I would make something happen.

Sackett's Land

. . . all change is difficult, all change is resisted, I think. No people can long remain in isolation, and men will go where there is land, it is their nature, as it is with animals, with plants, with all that lives.

Since the beginning of time men have moved across the face of the world, and we like to believe this is a result of our individual will, our choice, and it may be so, but might it not be that we are moved by tides buried in our natures? Tides we cannot resist?

To the Far Blue Mountains

A ship does not sail with yesterday's wind. . . .

The Walking Drum

There is but one thing we know . . . and that is that nothing forever remains the same.

Jubal Sackett

Nothing is gained without some risk. . . .

The Lonesome Gods

. . . I watched those in the room with me and was lonely within myself, for there was in me a great reaching outward, a desire to be and to become.

Bendigo Shafter

Even those who fancy themselves the most progressive will fight against other kinds of progress, for each of us is convinced that our way is the best way.

The Lonely Men

Each age is an age that is passing, and cities, my friend, are transitory things. Each is born from the dust; each matures, grows older, then it fades and dies. A passing traveler looks at a mound of sand and broken stones and asks, "What was here?" and his answer is only an echo or a wind drifting sand.

The Walking Drum

No man cuts himself free of old ties without regret; even scenes of hardship and sadness possess the warmth of familiarity, and within each of us there is a love for the known.

Lando

Who can read what is in tomorrow's wind?

To the Far Blue Mountains

I fear there will be no future for those who do not change. When there are no new ideas things can remain the same, but strangers are coming with different ways—

Jubal Sackett

When folks are making a fresh start they have to tolerate.

Bendigo Shafter

. . . we believe a man's destiny may be many things, although a way is prescribed, a man may change. It is interesting that so few do change.

The Walking Drum

Russia has so much to give, yet so much to learn. We should be a part of all that instead of being confined as in a prison. . . . But our growth is being stunted by restrictions and rules made by idiots defending themselves against the shadows that are only in their minds!

Last of the Breed

I knew it was upon her, too, that strangeness of returning, for the secret is what Shakespeare said, that no traveler returns. He is always a little changed, a little different, and wistful and longing for what has been lost.

Bendigo Shafter

The wind does not wait!

To the Far Blue Mountains

Civilization and Beliefs

Somehow I do not believe I shall be staying anywhere very long. Men and civilizations are alike, ma'am. They are born, they grow to strength, they mature, grow old, and die. It is the way of all things.

The Lonesome Gods

Civilization is simply an organization that man has developed in order that he may live in peace with his neighbors.

Last of the Breed

It is a thing I must remember, that men must always remember, that civilization is a flimsy cloak, and just outside are hunger, thirst, and cold . . . waiting.

Bendigo Shafter

Civilization is a trap for some men, a place of

glory for others. The mountains change with years, so must the Indian change.

Treasure Mountain

. . . it is not streets and buildings that make a town, but men and women.

Bendigo Shafter

A town can be more than one thing to men. It can be a process of education as well as a place to live and make a living. But to build anything and to make it last calls for discipline, the inner discipline that a man provides for himself and the cooperative discipline that men give to each other.

Bendigo Shafter

Few take the trouble to understand or to view the American scene with perspective. And we Americans love to find ourselves guilty of something. However, it is never I who am guilty, but those other Americans, the past or present government or the other political party. Americans almost never find other countries guilty. It is always ourselves or our fancied influence in other countries.

Last of the Breed

A man may not have much, but he sets store by his pride as a free-born American citizen, and is ready to fight for what he believes, you choose the time and place.

Chancy

The human eye has a readiness for patterns. Much is not seen simply because the mind is blind, not the eyes. The eyes see in lines, curves, and patterns. Man himself works in patterns simple or complex, and such things are often evidence of man's previous presence.

Treasure Mountain

. . . the more involved a civilization became the more vulnerable it became, and any disaster . . . can put man right back to the hunting and food-gathering level on which we now existed.

Bendigo Shafter

This here civilization we got is a mighty flimsy thing. There's laws, of course, but there's also an unspoken agreement among folks to abide by the rights of others. Anybody can make a mistake, but if he continues makin' that mistake he's shown himself unwilling to abide by the customs of others and so has no place in civilization.

Passin' Through

Maybe that was a part of what our town meant, maybe it was a place for . . . teaching a man to think not only of himself but of a community, a training ground for learning to live together, to think for others, to plan for a future.

Bendigo Shafter

There can be no living together without understanding, and understanding means compromise. Compromise is not a dirty word, it is the cornerstone of civilization, just as politics is the art of making civilization work.

Bendigo Shafter

A town means order, and order means law, and without them there can be no civilization, no peace, and no leisure. . . . the first culture and good living began when man learned to share the work and so provide leisure for music, for painting, for writing, and for study.

Bendigo Shafter

Evie . . . when in doubt, sit down and think. It is only the mind of man that has lifted him above the animals.

Conagher

To disbelieve is easy; to scoff is simple; to have faith is harder.

To the Far Blue Mountains

Nobody is ever convinced by argument. . . . They just think up new reasons for maintaining old positions and become more defensive.

Comstock Lode

Men need their gods, but did not the gods also need men?

The Lonesome Gods

All gods are useful. Who am I to say yours is not?

Jubal Sackett

Yet we readily accept the idea that a fat man is wise. Was he not wise enough to provide for himself? But we hesitate to ascribe piety to any but the lean. A fat prophet could never start a new religion, while a lean, ascetic-looking one could do it easily.

To the Far Blue Mountains

A prophet should always come down from the mountain or out of the desert. He should never arise from the table. . . .

To the Far Blue Mountains

Many are the paths to righteousness, and ours, I think, is but one.

The Warrior's Path

I have come to the mountains in doubt. I find them . . . I find them a place for the gods to walk.

Jubal Sackett

. . . when the scholars began to dig, it was to find familiar things. . . . Whatever they found tied into something, and when they found something strange, they shied from it because it would have no place, no connection.

The Lonesome Gods

Where we Sacketts come from in the high-up mountains of Tennessee, it is a known thing that if you sleep with a Bible under your pillow it will keep you safe from witches.

Mojave Crossing

My home is among the mountains. Men destroy what they do not understand, as they destroyed the son of God when he chose to walk among them. I do not wish to be understood. I wish to be left alone.

The Lonesome Gods

Man's civilization is . . . a thin barrier between man and his oldest enemy. Truly, man must be like the beaver, a building creature, only man must build cities as a beaver must build dams.

Bendigo Shafter

Perhaps . . . the spirit we worship is the same, and only the names are different. The message from He who rules over us all may come to each people in a different way.

Jubal Sackett

Each people has its gods, or the spirits in

which they believe. It may be their god is the same as ours, only clothed in different stories, different ideas, but a god can only be strong . . . if he is worshiped, and the gods of those ancient people are lonesome gods now.

The Lonesome Gods

History is not made only by kings and parliaments, presidents, wars, and generals. It is the story of people, of their love, honor, faith, hope and suffering; of birth and death, of hunger, thirst and cold, of loneliness and sorrow.

Sackett's Land

Knowledge, Education, and Learning

You are your own best teacher. My advice is to question all things. Seek for answers and when you find what seems to be an answer, question that, too.

The Walking Drum

There was a cowhand once who said that Shakespeare was the only poet who wrote like he'd been raised on red meat.

The Lonesome Gods

A mind, like a home, is furnished by its owner, so if one's life is cold and bare he can blame none but himself. You have a chance to select from some pretty elegant furnishings.

Bendigo Shafter

We needed books, we needed something on which to build dreams.

Ride the River

A man can learn a lot if he listens, and if I didn't learn anything else I was learning how much I didn't know.

The Daybreakers

. . . and you had a gift. . . . A gift of listening. When men spoke, you heard, and of what you heard, you thought.

Sackett's Land

What is wisdom? . . . I have often wondered, and I am not sure. Understanding of life and men, I presume. It goes beyond mere knowledge, as knowledge goes beyond information.

Last of the Breed

It is only the ignorant who can be positive, only the ignorant who can become fanatics, for the more I learned the more I became aware that there are shadings and relationships in all things.

The Walking Drum

Each of us must find wisdom in his own way. Mine is one way, yours another. Perhaps we each need more of what the other knows.

The Lonely Men

The little I have learned only shows me how very much there is to learn.

Bendigo Shafter

Sometimes I wonder if anything is ever ended. The words a man speaks today live on in his thoughts or the memories of others, and the shot fired, the blow struck, the thing done today is like a stone tossed into a pool and the ripples keep widening out until they touch lives far from ours.

The Daybreakers

Reading without thinking is as nothing, for a book is less important for what it says than for what it makes you think.

The Walking Drum

. . . the mind must be prepared for knowledge as one prepares a field for planting, and a discovery made too soon is no better than a discovery not made at all.

The Walking Drum

"My books have been the mountains," I said. "The desert, the forest, and the wide places where the grass grows."

The Lonely Men

Some folks think that being smart in the books is the only kind of smart, but that just isn't so. Men learn a lot by doin', and they learn by listenin' to what others say, but when a man is workin' on a farm or walkin' in the woods or ridin' across country, he can do a lot of thinking. Many a man who reads a lot just repeats what he's read, and not what he thinks.

Ride the River

Much can be learned from books, but much remains about which no book has been written. Remember this: the poor peasant, the hunter, or the fisherman may have knowledge that scholars are struggling to learn.

The Lonesome Gods

A school is wherever a man can learn, Mr. Shafter, do not forget that. A man can learn from these mountains and the trees, he can learn by listening, by seeing, and by hearing

63

the talk of other men and thinking about what they say.

Bendigo Shafter

They are only actors, you know, and much put upon. They are but shadows of the roles they play, and often there is only the shadow.

The Walking Drum

There is no curtain knowledge cannot penetrate, although the process can be slowed.

The Walking Drum

Much of what I say may be nonsense, but a few things I have learned, and the most important is that he who ceases to learn is already a half-dead man.

The Lonesome Gods

Honor first, then victory, but if a man is to learn, first he must live.

The Walking Drum

Is not yours the best way? To learn because one loves learning?

The Walking Drum

A man who is in love with learning is a man who is never without a bride, for there is always more.

Bendigo Shafter

An artist needs freedom, he needs innovation, he needs opportunity, he needs to create.

Last of the Breed

How young is too young to begin to discover the power and the beauty of words? Perhaps he will not understand, but there is a clash of shields and a call of trumpets in those lines. One cannot begin too young nor linger too long with learning.

The Lonesome Gods

To me the goal was to learn, to see, to know, to understand.

The Walking Drum

There are many who assume that once they have become men there is nothing to be learned from books.

The Lonesome Gods

Coming west in a wagon where every ounce of weight must be carefully judged, those who brought books brought the best, those which would stand continual rereading.

Comstock Lode

. . . I must have books, not only for our children but for Abigail and myself. We must not lose touch with what we were, with what we had been, nor must we allow the well of our history to dry up, for a child without tradition is a child crippled before the world. Tradition can also be an anchor of stability and a shield to guard one from irresponsibility and hasty decision.

To the Far Blue Mountains

Trusting in my strong right arm and my wits might all be very well, but I had so much to learn and knew not if either the arm or the wit was sufficient.

The Walking Drum

One lives so long to learn so little.

The Lonesome Gods

It is a poor sort of man who is content to be

66

spoon-fed knowledge that has been filtered through the canon of religious or political belief, and it is a poor sort of man who will permit others to dictate what he may or may not learn.

The Walking Drum

Sakim had taught me to be wary of evidence given by others, for in all evidence there is some interpretation. The eyes see, the mind explains. But does the mind explain correctly? The mind only has what experience and education have given it, and perhaps that is not enough. Because one has seen does not mean one knows.

Jubal Sackett

The more one learns the more he understands his ignorance. I am simply an ignorant man, trying to lessen his ignorance.

To the Far Blue Mountains

Much as I loved reading I was wary of it, for I soon saw that much that passed for thinking was simply a good memory, and many an educated man was merely repeating what he had learned, not what he had thought out for himself.

Bendigo Shafter

The only way folks got to where they are . . . was by thinkin' things out. No man ever had the claws of a grizzly nor the speed of a deer—what he had was a brain.

The Lonely Men

. . . all education is self-education. A teacher is only a guide, to point out the way, and no school, no matter how excellent, can give you an education.

The Lonesome Gods

It was my good fortune to have spoken first, a lesson to be remembered.

The Walking Drum

I have reverence for all who ask questions and seek honest answers.

The Walking Drum

Because a man doesn't speak good English doesn't mean he doesn't have good ideas.

Ride the River

What I shall seek tomorrow, I do not know. Today, I seek only to know. My mind asks questions for which I have no answers. Within me there is a loneliness for knowledge.

The Walking Drum

I never figured language was any stone-cold thing anyway. It's to provide meaning, to tell other folks what you have in mind, and there's no reason why if a man is short a word he can't invent one.

Galloway

There is power in the word whether written or spoken, for words can create images for those who have not themselves seen.

The Walking Drum

Men have passed on . . . knowledge . . . yet in politics, statecraft, and social relationships we continue to repeat old mistakes.

The Lonesome Gods

In knowledge lay not only power but freedom from fear, for generally speaking one only fears what one does not understand.

The Walking Drum

There were lessons I had yet to learn, and one was not to talk too much.

The Walking Drum

One never realizes how much and how little he knows until he starts talking.

Bendigo Shafter

. . . I seek when I can the company of others who learn, for who knows when my knowledge combined with theirs might prove the answer? Each man learns a little, but the sum of their knowledge can be great.

The Walking Drum

Knowledge was meant to be shared.

Jubal Sackett

A sword is never enough. The mind is also a weapon, but like the sword it must be honed and kept sharp.

The Walking Drum

Sometimes I think if it were not for books I could not live, I'd be so lonely. But I can take a book out of that trunk, and it is just like talking to an old friend, and I imagine them as they were, bent over their desks or tables, trying to put what they thought into words.

Bendigo Shafter

. . . we must read, not only for what we read but for what it makes us think.

The Warrior's Path

"Read much?"
"Now and again. A man alone gets hungry for some kind of communication, even if he's not a reader. I knew one who was snowed in one year, and when he came out with the spring thaw, he'd come so close to memorizing the Bible that he became a preacher."

Comstock Lode

Let God have his temples and cathedrals . . . if they will give us libraries!

The Walking Drum

. . . I wondered if in time man's brain might not become smaller, for as more knowledge was preserved in books or by other means, he might have to think less and contrive less.

Bendigo Shafter

Must one seek something? I seek to be seeking, as I learn to be learning. Each book is an adventure as is each day's horizon.

The Walking Drum

You have come into this world with good health and a good mind. The rest is up to you.

The Lonesome Gods

Money can be lost or stolen, health and strength may fail, but what you have committed to your mind is yours forever.

The Walking Drum

I should like to see this last because I have built it strong and made it good, but I know it will not. Even my books may not last, but the ideas will endure. It is easy to destroy a book, but an idea once implanted has roots no man can utterly destroy.

The Lonely Men

. . . no man has the right to be ignorant.

Sackett

Money, Wealth, and Poverty

The fact that I was about to pick up enough gold to make a man wealthy for life meant little when a body figured on it. What mattered was what a man made with his own hands, his own brains.

Mustang Man

A lot of people wish to find treasure, but few of them realize how hard it is to handle after you've got it.

Treasure Mountain

. . . gold is forever heavy.

To the Far Blue Mountains

Gold is a hard-kept secret.

The good, the bad, the strong, and the weak all flock to the kind of warmth that gold gives off.

Sackett

All things are valued according to their scarcity, and a time might come when this gift would seem as nothing. What was worth little to us was worth much to them because they were things they could not get elsewhere.

Jubal Sackett

Where there is gold . . . there is blood.
The Walking Drum

When it came to gold, I trusted nobody, not even myself. I'd never had much, and the sight of all that gold might turn me into a worse man than I figured to be.

Mustang Man

Gold is never a simple thing. Many a man has wished he had gold, but once he has it he finds trouble. Gold causes folks to lose their right thinking and their common sense. It had been lied for and killed for, and I was in a lawless land.

Sackett

I tell you, gold is easier found than kept.
Treasure Mountain

Sometimes even folks a body has figured were right good people have turned ugly when gold's in the picture.

Lonely on the Mountain

Evil comes often to a man with money; tyranny comes surely to him without it.

The Walking Drum

You think maybe having a mite more money will build a wall around you to keep you from what's creeping up on you, but it won't.

Treasure Mountain

Freedom first, then money. Freedom without money would simply make me a slave of another kind, a slave to a need for food, for shelter.

The Walking Drum

Hunger inspires no talent, and carried too far, it deadens the faculties and destroys initiative. . . .

The Walking Drum

Once you are in debt . . . you are carrying

another man's weight, and it will be him who sits in the saddle and his hands on the reins.

Comstock Lode

It is never too soon to learn how to handle money.

The Lonesome Gods

If people were sold only what they wanted, there would be little trade. . . . The soul of business is to inspire people to buy that which they neither want nor need.

The Walking Drum

. . . when one has possessions he is as often possessed by them as possessing them.

Jubal Sackett

Any time you find a lot of people who have to have something or do something you'll also find somebody there charging them for doing it.

Ride the Dark Trail

There were some poor folks up where we

come from, but they weren't poor in the things that make a man.

Lonely on the Mountain

He who had a sword could carve his way to wealth and power, and the kingdoms of the world were ruled by such men or their descendants.

The Walking Drum

Many people know how to get money, but few know how to keep it. Wise investments are always based on information. . . .

The Lonesome Gods

The dried leaves of autumn are lightly blown away, still more easily is the fortune of man destroyed.

The Walking Drum

It was in my mind to become rich in the western lands, but a body does not become rich tomorrow without starting today. . . .

Lando

Winning, Losing, and Luck

Luck comes to a man who puts himself in the way of it. You went where something might be found and you found something, simple as that.

To the Far Blue Mountains

Victory is not won in miles but in inches. Win a little now, hold your ground, and later win a little more.

The Walking Drum

To succeed as a human being is not always the same as succeeding in your life's work, although they can go hand in hand.

The Lonesome Gods

Trouble with me was, I was a mighty poor hater. There was satisfaction in winning, but

winning would have been better if nobody
had to lose.

Lando

Sometimes I think it is not the money, but
the game. It isn't the winning so much as it
is to play the cards right.

Comstock Lode

Nothing in my nature permitted me to trust
to fortune, for it was my belief that good
luck came to those who work hard and plan
well.

To the Far Blue Mountains

Winning can make folks confident . . . or it
can make them cautious.

The Sky-Liners

The Frontier

A man has to blaze his own trail, and mine was to the west.

Jubal Sackett

People who live in comfortable, settled towns with law-abiding citizens and a government to protect them, they never think of the men who came first, the ones who went through hell to build something.

Sackett

Settled folks always look down upon the unsettled . . . but somebody has to open the new lands.

Ride the River

Men like to believe themselves free from nature, free of the drives that move animals and plants, but wherever there is open space men will come to occupy it.

To the Far Blue Mountains

The frontier asked no questions and gave its rewards to the strong.

The Daybreakers

My folks built blood into the foundations of this country and I don't aim to see them torn down for no reason whatsoever.

Sackett

Folks on the frontier hadn't any secret sins. . . . On the frontier the country was too wide, there was too much open space for a body to be able to cover anything up.

The Sackett Brand

We who wandered the land knew this was no "new world." The term was merely a conceit in the minds of those who had not known of it before.

Jubal Sackett

. . . we white men in striving for our success, in seeking to build a new world from what lies about us, sometimes forget there are other ways, sometimes forget the Lonesome Gods of the far places, the gods who live on the empty sea, who dance with the dust devils and who wait quietly in the shadows under the cliffs where ancient men have marked their passing with hands.

The Lonesome Gods

The call of the horizon finds quick response in the heart of every wanderer.

The Walking Drum

I began to see that the westward movement, the pioneer movement, had been a selective process, and that those who came west were possessed of something distinctive, for better or worse. More courage? Well . . . possibly. Some primitive throwback to the times of migration? . . . Why did some go and others stay? . . . . No movement in history was like it . . . Possibly the only motivating force, understood or not, was a love of freedom for its own sake.

Bendigo Shafter

About all he'd ever had out of life was a seat in a saddle and a lot of open country to look at.

Conagher

. . . we who pass do not own this land, we but use it, we hold it briefly in trust for those yet to come. We must not reap without seeding, we must not take from the earth without replacing.

The Lonesome Gods

Had I done nothing else, I left them this birthright . . . for I knew that out there beyond the great river, beyond the wide plain, beyond the shining mountains . . . beyond . . . there would be, for the men of this land, forever a beyond.

To the Far Blue Mountains

I have been nothing . . . but there is tomorrow.

The Walking Drum

Some will go further and further back into the hills until they can go no further, some will fall by the way, but a good many will move out into this new world, and they will do well.

Bendigo Shafter

. . . the greatest myth is that of the discovery

of any country, for all countries were known in the long ago, and all seas sailed in times gone by.

To the Far Blue Mountains

. . . against the western sky there were mountains, blue and distant mountains. I must pass through them. I must see what lies beyond.

Sackett's Land

. . . if you hadn't come along the old boy would have been dead by now. You took him along, you asked his advice, and suddenly he had a reason for living, he was riding the trail again.

Bendigo Shafter

They like it strong out there. They say if you can't float a horseshoe on it the coffee is too weak.

Conagher

To live in a city, one must be larger than one's environment or enjoy belonging to the crowd. Out here a person can become a part of it all. He can walk the heights with the eagles and the clouds, but it needs a special kind of person.

The Lonesome Gods

And there remains with us the feeling that we can move again, that there is always a better place somewhere out beyond the rim of the world.

Bendigo Shafter

"You are a hero!"

"It is an empty word out here, ma'am. It is a word for writers and sitters by the fire. Out here a man does what the situation demands. Out on the frontier we do not have heroes, only people doing what is necessary at the time."

The Lonesome Gods

Tye, this is big country out here and it takes big men to live in it, but it gives every man an equal opportunity. You're just as big or small as your vision is, and if you've a mind to work and make something of yourself, you can do it.

The Daybreakers

. . . my star hung over the western mountains and I knew it.

Jubal Sackett

Yol bolsun! . . . May there be a road! (Turkish greeting)

The Walking Drum

. . . I was just thinking of how wonderful it was to be riding west into a new land, and to be sleeping under the stars.

The Lonesome Gods

The promised land is always a distant land, aglow with golden fire. It is a land one never attains, for once attained one faces fulfillment and the knowledge that whatever a land may promise, it may also demand a payment of courage and strength.

Bendigo Shafter

All I know is that I shall never rest easy until I have gone into the desert alone. Until I have followed some of those trails to wherever they go.

The Lonesome Gods

We need such men, lad, men who can look to the beyond, to ever strive for something out there beyond the stars. It is man's destiny, I think, to go forward, ever forward. We are of the breed, you and I, the breed who venture always toward what lies out there—westward, onward, everward.

The Warrior's Path

Indians

Injuns don't think the same as us, and we keep thinkin' they do. That's been the cause of most of the trouble. We think one way, they think another, and even when the words are the same, they mean different things.

Lonely on the Mountain

What is a savage? . . . It is another way of life.

Sackett's Land

We do wrong . . . to try to convert them to our beliefs. First we should study what they believe and how it applies to the way they live.

The Lonesome Gods

Only to say there were many paths, all directed to the same end, and he advised me not to be too quick to put my religion upon the Indian, for he had one of his own that served him well.

The Warrior's Path

The ethics of the white man are his own, and contrary to what he may believe, are not shared by others. Not in all cases, at least. Each people has its own standards, often similar, yet with notable differences.

Bendigo Shafter

If I make one last prayer I ask that your god grant me an enemy. If I have an enemy, even one enemy, I can be strong.

Jubal Sackett

As they must fight with their enemies, they respect a fighter. As a coward is a danger to them, they despise a coward.

To the Far Blue Mountains

. . . a lot of virtues they were given credit for by white men were only ideas in a white man's head, and no Indian would have considered them virtues. Mercy rarely had any part in the make-up of an Indian. . . . folks who are brought up to Christian ways of thought don't believe in the taking of life, but the Indian had no such conception.

Sackett

Mercy is a taught thing. Nobody comes by it natural. Indians grew up thinking the tribe was all there was and anybody else was an enemy.

It wasn't a fault, simply that nobody had ever suggested such a thing to him. An enemy was to be killed, and then cut up so if you met him in the afterlife he wouldn't have the use of his limbs to attack you again. . . .

Indians respect a fighter and they respect almost nobody else. But sometimes they cut them up, too.

The Daybreakers

Apaches are great waiters. They could set for hours on end, just waiting a wrong move. A white man, he gets restless, wants to move, and the first thing you know he does, and he dies.

The Lonely Men

The Indian is a great hunter and as such he has patience, yet my life in the wilderness had taught me patience also. One learns to adapt to the land in which one lives.

Jubal Sackett

Learn from the Indians . . . but with them one must always be strong. They respect truth, and they respect strength.

The Lonesome Gods

The white man has driven out the Indian, but the Indian drove out others before, and those others had driven peoples before them.

The Lonely Men

They had observed white men traveling in the cold and had seen them muffle their ears with ear laps, turn coat collars up to narrow their vision, and huddle deep into their coats, seeking nothing but warmth. Sometimes it is better to be a little cold and remain alive.

Bendigo Shafter

They fought as strong men fight, for the love of battle and because fighting is a part of the life they live.

Treasure Mountain

Indians . . . do not frighten easily. War is their way of life.

Jubal Sackett

The Indian in his native land did not seek for material wealth. He hunted, gathered, and lived. What he sought was stronger medicine, greater wisdom, a power within him that could equal the power of the spirits that surrounded him and could endanger him if he could not enlist their aid.

Jubal Sackett

Yet when two peoples come together that one which is most efficient will survive, and the other will absorb or vanish . . . it is the way of life.

The Indian must not lose pride in what he does, in his handicraft, for if he loses pride he will no longer build, his art will fail him, and he will completely be dependent upon others.

Sackett's Land

They respect courage. You can't yield to an Indian. He will kill you out of contempt as much as for any other reason, but he respects courage, and he respects a good argument.

Conagher

Dealing with Indians I found them of shrewd intelligence, quick to detect the false, quick to appreciate quality, quick to resent contempt and to appreciate bravery. So much of the Indian's life was predicated upon courage that he respected it above all else. He needed courage in the hunt, and in warfare, and to achieve success within the tribe he needed both courage and wit.

Sackett's Land

An Indian boy is not a man until he is a warrior. To be a warrior he must fight, take scalps, count coup. And they do not forget old enmities.

To the Far Blue Mountains

Medicine to an Indian means power, and his life is spent in seeking the right medicine. He wishes for strong medicine for himself and those he follows, and he fears it in the possession of others.

Jubal Sackett

The Indian lived a life that demanded courage, demanded strength, stamina, and the will to survive; and the white men who came first to the mountains had such qualities—or they would not have come in the first place, and they could not have lasted in the second.

Treasure Mountain

Honor, the Law, and Justice

. . . if men are to survive upon the earth there must be law, and there must be justice and all men must stand together against those who would strike at the roots of what men have so carefully built.

The Lonesome Gods

You know what you respect and what you do not, so all that is left is to weigh each law, each idea against what you know, decide how you would like things to be, and then work to make them so.

To the Far Blue Mountains

You asked if I have reverence? I have reverence for truth, but I do not know what truth is. I suspect there are many truths, and therefore, I suspect all who claim to have *the* truth.

The Walking Drum

Maybe I don't agree with the government on all things, but we elected them, a majority of us did, and it's up to us to stand by them and their laws.

Lonely on the Mountain

A lawman . . . is not a restraint, but a freedom, a liberation. He restrains only those who would break the laws and provides freedom for the rest of us to work, to laugh, to sing, to play in peace.

Bendigo Shafter

A man can compromise to gain a point. . . . Remember this . . . even a rebel grows old, and sometimes wiser. He finds the things he rebelled against are now the things he must defend against newer rebels. . . . Be discreet, but follow your own mind. When you have obtained position you will have influence. Otherwise you will tear at the bars until your strength is gone, and you will have accomplished nothing but to rant and rave.

The Walking Drum

Long ago I heard a man in the country store near my home say that a just man always had doubts.

Ride the Dark Trail

There is no greater role for a man to play than to assist in the government of a people, nor anyone lower than he who misuses that power.

The Lonesome Gods

When a man enters into society . . . he agrees to abide by the rules of that society, and when he crosses those rules he becomes liable to judgment, and if he continues to cross them, then he becomes an outlaw.

Sackett

. . . governments may change, but a people do not, nor does their basic thinking change.

The Lonesome Gods

Honor is the thing, for he who is honorable needs no praise. He is secure with the knowledge of what he is, a decent human being first, all else after.

The Walking Drum

The worst of it was, he was a very good gambler, and when one is successful there is always a question of one's honesty.

Bendigo Shafter

Everyone hopes for an immediate solution, but the only solutions to social problems come through time. We in America always believe we have only to pass a law and everything will be changed. . . . People only obey a law the majority have already decided to obey, and it must be a very large majority.

Bendigo Shafter

I've a regard for the law, although I do not always agree with it.

Sackett's Land

. . . that where man was, there must be law, for without it man descends to less than he is, certainly less than he can become.

The Warrior's Path

We have hedged ourselves round with law, for we know that if man is to survive it must be through cooperative effort.

The Lonesome Gods

. . . honor is important only when dealing with honorable men.

The Walking Drum

. . . it takes more than owning a lot of cows to make a big man. Hanging anybody you can find or anybody you don't like makes you nothing but a murderer, lower than any of the men you chase.

Ride the Dark Trail

Betters? Who is better unless he makes himself so? You can be one of those for whom laws are made if you so will it, or you can be a maker of laws yourself.

To the Far Blue Mountains

Often . . . I find it best to do what must be done without going through the usual channels.

The Warrior's Path

I suspect those gentlemen up the street have already selected their twelve jurymen, and they are in the chambers of their pistols.

Lonely on the Mountain

. . . there's nothing in this world I can't get without lying or cheating.

The Daybreakers

Yet it is honor I wish for them, honor and pride of person, not wealth.

To the Far Blue Mountains

I want my son to learn what he can, but most of all I wish him to be a citizen, to judge issues, to use logic in his thinking, to respect his country and its people.

Bendigo Shafter

Honor can be a troublesome thing, but if one has it one does not lightly yield it.

The Walking Drum

Lie to a liar, for lies are his coin; steal from a thief, for that is easy; lay a trap for the trickster and catch him at the first attempt, but beware of an honest man. (Somali saying)

The Walking Drum

. . . if the folks who believe in law, justice, and a decent life for folks are to be shot down by those who believe in violence, nothing makes much sense.

Sackett

Wild Places, Wild Life

I think I am in this world to find beauty in lonely places.

Jubal Sackett

Ma'am . . . I don't know what it is you are wishful for in this life, but you set down of a night and you pray to God that he'll let you walk alone across a mountain meadow when the wild flowers are blooming.

You pray he'll let you set by a mountain stream with sunlight falling through the aspens, or that he'll let you ride across an above-timberline plateau with the strong bare peaks around you and the black thunderheads gathering around them—great, swelling rain clouds ready to turn the meadows into swamp in a minute or two . . . you let him show you those things, ma'am, and you'll never miss heaven if you don't make it.

Treasure Mountain

A big country can breed big men.

Bendigo Shafter

I walk in the shoes of the men of today. I fly their planes, I eat their food, but my heart is in the wilderness with feathers in my hair.

Last of the Breed

Man is not long from the wilderness, and it takes him but a short time to go back to living with it. . . .

To the Far Blue Mountains

You can't fight the desert . . . you have to ride with it.

The Lonely Men

This desert is a book of many pages, and just when you believe you know all there is to know, it will surprise you with the unexpected.

The Lonesome Gods

The desert and the wild country taught me not only to look, but to see . . . and there is a difference.

Bendigo Shafter

Every step a man takes in desert country has to be taken with water in mind.

The Lonely Men

That's desert! Real ol' desert! But let me tell you somethin'! It's been called "hell with the fires out," an' that's a fair description, but there's life out there, boy! Life! You can live with the desert if you learn it. You can live with it, live in it, live off of it, but you got to do it the desert's way an' you got to know the rules.

But never take it lightly, son! If you do, she'll rise right up, an' the next thing you know, the wind is playin' music in your ribs and honin' your skull with sand.

The Lonesome Gods

To truly know the mountains, one should go to meet them as one would meet a sweetheart, alone.

Last of the Breed

If a body takes out to follow a made trail down over the hills, he'd best hold to that trail, for there are not too many ways to go. Most of the trouble a man finds in the mountains is when he tries shortcuts or leaves a known way.

Treasure Mountain

A mountain man tries to live with the country instead of against it.

Sackett

When I look at those mountains, I see the centuries pass like seasons.

The Lonesome Gods

I want to come out of a morning and look up at those hills and know nothing can be very wrong as long as there's something so beautiful.

Galloway

My pa used to say that when corruption is visited upon the cities of men, the mountains and the deserts await him. The cities are for money but the high-up hills are purely for the soul.

Galloway

Now the mountain was stark and beautiful, a place for no man or animal, just for the clouds and eagles.

Jubal Sackett

"Until then, Laban, you can read the land."

"The land?"

"Look upon the land, Laban—there are stories everywhere. Study the sky and the trees, the tracks of animals and the way the birds fly. You can learn things no book will ever teach you."

Conagher

Darkness made a mystery of the forest and goblins of the trees.

Lonely on the Mountain

The air was incredibly clear. Fresh and cool as it was, one breathed in it like drinking cool water; and always there was a definite odor on it, the odor depending on the direction from which the wind blew: the smell of cedar, and of pines beyond, the smell of sage, or, from the dryer lands after a rain, the smell of the creosote bush.

Conagher

A man living in wild country develops a sense of the rightness of things . . . and he becomes like an animal in sensing when all is not well. . . .

Against such men you never ride easy in the saddle, you make your plans, you figure things out, and then you are careful. I never knew a really brave man yet who was reckless, nor did I ever know a real fighting man who was reckless . . . maybe because the reckless ones were all dead.

The Daybreakers

No animal has any special respect for man. . . . It is just that they have learned to fear. Once they lose their fear, a man has to be careful.

The Lonesome Gods

There is a saying among my people that the deer may forget the snare, but the snare does not forget the deer.

The Walking Drum

Men and animals form habits. They have certain ways of doing things, and once you have visited a camp or two you always know how that man will camp again.

Last of the Breed

There's nothing you could offer me that I'd

swap for one afternoon ride through the hills, and I mean it. Once a man has lived with mountains you can't offer him a home with a prairie dog.

Treasure Mountain

How many times have I talked with people who have ridden the trails where I have ridden, yet had seen nothing? They passed over the land just to get over it, not to live with it and see it, feel it.

Bendigo Shafter

The thing to remember when traveling is that the trail is the thing, not the end of the trail. Travel too fast and you miss all you are traveling for.

Ride the Dark Trail

It was a rough, hard land, and we learned to walk careful and keep our eyes open, trusting in the Lord and a fast gunhand.

Chancy

He'll [a woodsman] have in his mind many possible camps that he'll never have time to use, and he'll notice tangles to avoid, things a man might trip over, and bad footing generally. After a time a man takes all these things in without really thinking about it. But if something is out of place he will see it instantly.

Treasure Mountain

Get hold of some land. It will last and be there when all the rest has changed. Everything else fades with time, but the land stays there.

The Lonesome Gods

A man living in wild country has to be aware of everything around him.

The Lonely Men

How big a man is depends on how big a territory he's in.

Passin' Through

It was a wild, lonely country with occasional streamers of snow in the shadows where the sun did not reach. The wind was cold off the mountains and I was a naked man with enemies behind me and nothing before me but hope.

Galloway

Out there where the forest brushes the sky, that's my kind of country.

Ride the River

The Sacketts are an odd lot. . . . No sooner did they get ashore in this country than they headed for the hills. Like homing pigeons. Once there, they took to the wilderness as if born to it.

Ride the River

. . . skilled tracking is a mark of a great hunter and a great warrior.

Jubal Sackett

Always take your bearings. Locate yourself.

The Lonesome Gods

A man riding wild country keeps his eyes open for camping places. He may not need one at that spot on the way out, but it might be just what the doctor ordered on the way back.

Treasure Mountain

A man who travels wild country gets to studying where he's coming from, because some day he might have to go back, and a trail looks a lot different when you ride over it in the opposite direction.

Mojave Crossing

A wild animal is not likely to step on a twig or branch out in the trees and brush. Only a man, or sometimes a horse or cow, will do that, but usually when a branch cracks somewhere it is a man moving, and every man in that camp would know it.

The Sky-Liners

He was a good cutting horse who could turn on a dime and have six cents left. . . .

The Sky-Liners

In the western lands a man had best be good friends with his horse or he may never have another friend or need of one. A man afoot in wild country is a man who may not live out the day . . . which is why horse-stealing was the major sin.

Galloway

. . . a wild horse has all the senses of a deer and a good deal more savvy.

Ride the Dark Trail

110

That man's gone loco like an old buffalo bull who's left the herd.

The Daybreakers

My mouth was dry as the inside of an old packrat's nest. . . .

The Lonesome Gods

. . . he looked as cheerful as a 'possum eatin' persimmons.

Mojave Crossing

Eastern folks might call this adventure, but it is one thing to read of an adventure sitting in an easy chair with a cool drink at hand, and quite another thing to be belly down in the hot dust with four, five Indians coming up the slope at you with killing on their minds.

The Daybreakers

He was a man of no patience; you could see it in him. That was a notch against him. In the wild country, a body needs patience.

Ride the River

I'd been on the trail for a long while, and a man tires faster when his nerves are on edge.

When you're hunting and being hunted, every fiber of your being is poised and ready.
Treasure Mountain

To pursue a man effectively, it is best to begin with his thinking.
Last of the Breed

We who walk the woodland paths know that although all men look, not many see. It is not only to keep the eyes open but to see what is there and to understand.
The Warrior's Path

All about them were conditions and circumstances to which they must adjust, attack by Indians or outlaw trappers was an ever-present danger, they lived on the very knife-edge of reality, and when this is so, the mind becomes a beautifully tuned instrument.
The Lonesome Gods

It was good to sit quiet a moment and look upon the land, for the flowers were out and it was carpeted with beauty. Little enough time I had for that, but it came to me through the air I breathed, for the loveliness of this

112

land was always with one who traveled through it.

The Sackett Brand

My father had fled to the hills, had lost himself out there where the silent gods awaited, eyes hollow with loneliness for the worshipers they no longer had. Out there under the sky, under the stars by night, they waited for the click of a stone thrown upon a pile, for arms lifted in prayer.

The Lonesome Gods

It is an old custom of these people to pick up a stone and toss it on the pile. Perhaps it is a symbolical lightening of the load they carry, perhaps a small offering to the gods of the trails.

The Lonesome Gods

Sometimes a man's senses will pick up sounds or glimpses not strong enough to make an impression on him, but they affect his thinking anyway. Maybe that's all there is to instinct or the awareness a man develops when he's in dangerous country. One thing I do know, his senses become tuned to sounds above and below the usual ranges of hearing.

The Daybreakers

She had believed the land was her enemy, and she struggled against it, but you could not make war against a land any more than you could against the sea. One had to learn to live with it, to belong to it, to fit into its seasons and its ways.

The land was a living thing, breathing with the wind, weeping with the rain, growing somber with clouds or gay with sunlight.

Conagher

I know what lies beyond your mountains, and it is only more mountains. Beyond each bend in the road there is another bend in the road. You may go, but I shall sit in a tavern and drink the wine of the land, of whatever land, and pinch the girls of the country and perhaps be slapped for my pinching, but be smiled at, too.

Sackett's Land

"But you do not know what music is until you have heard the wind in the cedars, or the far-off wind in the pines. Someday I am going to get on a horse and ride out there"— she pointed toward the wide grass before them—"until I can see the other side . . . if there is another side."

Conagher

. . . after the sun goes down. The glare is gone, everything is still, and things sort of stand out. Sound carries further and any movement is easier seen. You put that away in your skull an' hold it for another time.

The Lonesome Gods

Mountains are hard upon evil. . . . They don't hold with it.

Treasure Mountain

. . . for when the trees are gone, man will also be gone, for without them we cannot live.

The Lonesome Gods

Isn't that what we're all hunting for? A green valley somewhere?

Chancy

This was a land for me, these mountains, this forest, these silent streams, their voices stilled only for the time.

Jubal Sackett

Yet we must never forget that the land and the waters are ours for the moment only, that generations will follow who must themselves live from that land and drink that water. It would not be enough to leave something for them; we must leave it all a little better than we found it.

The Lonesome Gods

Trust

Trust yourself. You know this country. If you're uneasy, there's a reason. Your senses have perceived something your brain hasn't.
The Lonesome Gods

Be wary . . . of trusting too much. Men change and times change, but wars and revolutions are always with us.
To the Far Blue Mountains

Most folks can be trusted up to a point, but it always seemed to me the best thing was not to put temptation in their way.
Mojave Crossing

One should never trust anyone too much. . . . I'm a quiet man, and I'm much alone, but despite that, I like people. At the same time I know we are all subject to temptation and we are all human and you can always find excuses for what you do.

Comstock Lode

Begin to depend on no one but yourself. The fewer people whom you trust, the fewer on whom you rely, the better for you. Especially when traveling.

Bendigo Shafter

It behooves one to be wary when among strangers and not to trust too much.

Jubal Sackett

A man who starts imagining that others think good because he does is simply out of his mind.

Galloway

It always seemed to me that a man who would betray the trust of his fellow citizens is the lowest of all. . . .

Lando

Be friendly with all men and censure none, tell nobody too much of your affairs and remember in all dealings with men, or women, to keep one hand upon the door latch . . . in your mind, at least.

To the Far Blue Mountains

Men and Bravery

He was the kind if you got in trouble you didn't look to see if he was still with you— you knew damned well he was.

Sackett

What men call a hero . . . is merely a man who is seen doing what a brave man does as a matter of course.

Bendigo Shafter

I've nothing against a man being scared as long as he does what has to be done . . . being scared can keep a man from getting killed and often makes a better fighter of him.

The Daybreakers

It is good to say that you are afraid. . . . It is not good to be too bold. A little fear makes a

120

man think. It is better to be a little afraid, and yet do what has to be done.

Sackett's Land

Yet each move one makes is a risk, and if one thinks too long one does not move at all, for fear of what may come, and so becomes immobile, crouched in a shell, fearful of any move.

To the Far Blue Mountains

This was raw, open country, rugged country, and it bred a different kind of man. . . . it bred the kind of man with guts and toughness no eastern man could use.

Most men never discover what they've got inside. A man has to face up to trouble before he knows.

The Daybreakers

It is better . . . to fear a little. One is cautious then.

The Warrior's Path

I've learned that fear can be one's first line of defense. One has to be aware of danger to defend oneself against it.

Comstock Lode

. . . I knew the dangers a coward can offer, for his fear will often drive him to kill more quickly than if he were a brave man.

The Walking Drum

A man who says he has never been scared is either lying or else he's never been any place or done anything.

Sackett

A man needs heroes. He needs to believe in strength, nobility, and courage. Otherwise we become sheep to be herded to the slaughterhouse of death. I believe this. I am a soldier. I try to fight for the right cause. Sometimes it is hard to know.

But I do not sit back and sneer in cowardice at those with the courage to fight. The blood of good men makes the earth rich, as it is here. When I die sword in hand, I hope someone lives to sing of it. I live my life so that when death comes I may die well. I ask no more.

Sackett's Land

It was said of the young buck deer when his horns were fresh and in velvet that he was a "greenhorn," for he was foolishly brave then, ready to challenge anything. . . . So the name greenhorn was given to anyone young and braver than he had a right to be. . . .

The Sky-Liners

To be reckless is not to be brave, it is only to be a fool.

The Walking Drum

A man who can shoot like you can . . . isn't likely to have anybody question the way he signs his name.

Sackett

I did not doubt his courage, but there is a time to be brave and a time not to be a damned fool.

Lonely on the Mountain

Did you ever buck a man who just plain don't care? Everybody dies but him.

Galloway

Those were tough men . . . and a tough man with a will to live is a hard man to kill.

Chancy

A man out here who speaks careless of others will soon only have a marker in the graveyard.

The Lonesome Gods

I dare say anything . . . because I have a fast horse.

The Walking Drum

Courage comes cheap when you've got a man hog-tied.

The Sackett Brand

When I was a small boy I often went to the woods to lie on the grass in the shade. Somehow I had come to believe the earth could give me wisdom, but it did not. Yet I learned a little about animals and learned it is not always brave to make a stand. It is often foolish. There is a time for courage and a time for flight.

Ride the Dark Trail

A man shares his days with hunger, thirst, and cold, with the good times and the bad, and the first part of being a man is to understand that.

Galloway

When a body sets out to find another man's trail, he has to sort of ease his way into that man's thoughts and try to reason out what he might have done.

Treasure Mountain

I have observed . . . that the steps of a man sound heavier when he is alone in the hall.

The Walking Drum

In those days, when you said somebody was a bad man you did not mean that he was necessarily an evil man. It might just mean that he was a bad man to tangle with.

Chancy

The trouble with having a reputation as a tough man is that the time always comes when you have to be a tough man. It's a whole lot different.

The Daybreakers

Maybe I was young but I'd already learned a few things, and one of them was that if you throw your weight around somebody is going to call your hand . . . and he might be a whole sight tougher and meaner than you.

Bendigo Shafter

He explained to me . . . there was within people a fear of anything different than themselves. It was a deep-seated, primitive fear found among many wild creatures. A white wolf to exist among gray wolves must become a fierce fighter or be killed. It is a fear, perhaps, of attracting attention and therefore danger.

The Lonesome Gods

They feared what they did not understand.
The Walking Drum

A man who travels alone must look out for himself.

Lando

. . . when a man faces a man's problems he has to face them a man's way.

Sackett

Think . . . and act with coolness. Do what must be done.

The Lonesome Gods

. . . there was nothing a man couldn't get out of if he was sober and didn't panic. . . .

Galloway

He never backed off from trouble.

Conagher

. . . Do not be afraid. A little fear can make one cautious. Too much fear can rob you of initiative. Respect fear, but use it for an incentive, do not let it bind you or tie you down.

The Lonesome Gods

A knife is sharpened on stone, steel is tempered by fire, but men must be sharpened by men.

The Walking Drum

Caution always, but when a man acts he should act suddenly and with decision.

The Walking Drum

Anyway, it never does a man much good to be thinking of what he could do if he had help . . . better spend his time figuring a way of doing it himself.

Sackett

Alone I was, but he who stands alone is

often the strongest. By standing alone he becomes stronger and remains strong.

The Walking Drum

It is men who make a town, and bigger men who make a city.

The Lonesome Gods

In this country . . . a man saddles his own broncos and settles his own difficulties.

Lando

. . . a man who has to ask for help better not start out in the first place.

Conagher

From time to time he thought of moving on, of going to some other area . . . but his good sense told him things would be no better there than here. To keep moving was to try to escape from a problem he carried with him.

Comstock Lode

. . . and he is brave, indeed, who fears but does what must be done despite it.

The Walking Drum

Appearances count for little, and I knew I must shape the character of the man I wished to be into something of worth.
The Walking Drum

"There are good men everywhere."
"I only wish they had louder voices."
Last of the Breed

God help us always to have them, men who believe in what they are doing, and who will fight for what they believe.
To the Far Blue Mountains

. . . often have I wondered what it is that starts the drum of a man's life to beating? For each of us walks to the beat of our own drum, an unheard rhythm of all our movements and thought.
The Walking Drum

Many a man thinks large of himself because he doesn't know the company he's in. No matter how good a man can get at anything, there's always a time when somebody comes along who's better.
Lonely on the Mountain

These, Master, are the virtues of a man. . . .
That he has traveled far, for travel brings
wisdom; that he speak well to speak well of
what he has seen; and that he can fight, to
whip the man who doubts his stories!

The Walking Drum

One thing we learned. To make a start and
keep plugging. When I had fights at school,
the little while I went, I just bowed my neck
and kept swinging until something hit the
dirt. Sometimes it was me, but I always got
up.

Galloway

He was a square-jawed man, and I found
that he had a blunt, whimsical way about
him. He glanced up at me. "The marshal is
out," he said. "If you want to leave a message, just whistle it and I'll try to remember
the tune."

Chancy

A bulky, heavy man, was it fat or muscle?
Some of the most powerful men he had ever
seen looked fat.

Comstock Lode

. . . Trust to your wits, boy, and to your good right hand.

. . . And if you've a good left and some gold, that helps, too!

The Walking Drum

Any man can shoot a gun, and with practice he can draw fast and shoot accurately, but that makes no difference. What counts is how you stand up when somebody is shooting back at you.

Sackett

. . . a riding man is always better thinking off by himself.

Treasure Mountain

I spoke aloud, as a lonely man often does, hungry for the sound of some voice, even if it is his own.

The Lonesome Gods

Now the three of them were chancing their lives to lend me a hand; but that was the way with western men, and chances were I'd have done the same for them.

The Lonely Men

There is no man more dangerous than one who does not doubt his own rightness.

Ride the Dark Trail

Neither age nor size makes a man. . . .

The Lonesome Gods

. . . Men like to talk of what concerns them. Learn to listen, and if you can ask a question now and again, do it. Give them those big eyes of yours and you'll have no problem. You'll be bored often enough, but you'll learn a lot, too, and they will go away telling everybody what a charmin' girl you are.

Ride the River

A man should trust his senses and they'll grow sharper from use.

The Daybreakers

There is no miraculous change that takes place in a boy that makes him a man. He becomes a man by being a man. . . .

The Walking Drum

It is the willingness to accept responsibility, I think, that is the measure of a man.

Bendigo Shafter

"I saw him and I liked what I saw, a very dangerous man but a *man,* and I had a feeling if he gave his word it would prove good."

"You gave him something that meant more than anything else could. You trusted him and you respected him. His kind of man wants little else."

Comstock Lode

You've one hand and two eyes, and you look to have been a sharp man. Such a man should find something he can do, can make, can be. If you quit at this, it's because you've no guts in you.

The Warrior's Path

In the end it is up to the man what he becomes, and none of those other things matter. In horses, dogs, and men it is character that counts.

Chancy

A man can carve from stone, he can write fine words, or he can do something to hold himself in the hearts of people.

Treasure Mountain

He never knew when he was whipped . . .
so he never was.

Sackett's Land

Power and Strength

Strength never made right, and it is an indecency when it is allowed to breed corruption.

The Daybreakers

If strength could not win, one must use wit, if one has any.

Jubal Sackett

Authority, in this world in which I moved, implied belief in and acceptance of a dogma, and dogma is invariably wrong, as knowledge is always in a state of transition. The radical ideas of today are often the conservative policies of tomorrow, and dogma is left protesting by the wayside.

The Walking Drum

Powerful friends could make armor of a word, and from their lips a phrase could be a shield.

The Walking Drum

Men strive for peace, but it is their enemies that give them strength, and I think if man no longer had enemies, he would have to invent them, for his strength only grows from struggle.

The Lonesome Gods

The weak can be terrible when they wish to appear strong, and he was such a man, darkly vengeful and unforgetting. If dying, he would strike out wickedly in all directions to injure all he could to his last breath.

The Walking Drum

It is not enough . . . to own property in these days. One must be strong enough to keep it. If one is not strong, then there is no hope.

The Daybreakers

To talk too much is always a fault. Information is power.

Jubal Sackett

A king must think not only of today . . . but of tomorrow and tomorrow. When a law is passed, he must understand its consequences.

Moreover, he must always think of the succession.

To the Far Blue Mountains

The mob always wishes to make its hero the emperor, but no sooner is he emperor than they have another hero they wish in his place.

The Walking Drum

The favors of great men or women are like blushes on the cheeks of a courtesan—rare, nice to see, but not to be relied upon.

The Walking Drum

Her fear gave me strength, for when is one not the stronger through being needed?

The Walking Drum

. . . any obstacle can do the same. Anything that makes one struggle to be stronger, to be better.

Jubal Sackett

Many a small man is considered good while he remains small, but let power come to him, and he becomes a raging fury.

The Walking Drum

You have made a powerful enemy, but a man may be judged by who his enemies are, and their power.

The Walking Drum

The spirit of a strong man does not easily break, but he must be inwardly strong, secure in his beliefs and in what he is.

The Walking Drum

Violence and Crime

A man who wishes to kill . . . must also be ready to die.

The Walking Drum

Most people have no understanding or expectation of violence. They read of it in newspapers or books but it doesn't touch them. They've no realization of how vicious and murderous some people can be, or what they are prepared to do for money. And it did not have to be a lot of money.

Passin' Through

When somebody tries to make it with a gun, he has already admitted he hasn't the guts to make it the honest way. Whether he realizes it or not, life has already whipped him. From there on, it's all downhill.

The Hills of Homicide

When one man takes a gun and sets out to rob another, maybe to kill in the process, he should expect no sympathy.

Comstock Lode

No man in his right mind will play with a gun. I've seen show-offs doing fancy spins and all that. No real gun-fighter ever did. With a hairtrigger, he'd be likely to blow a hole in his belly.

The Sky-Liners

Violence is an evil thing, but when the guns are all in the hands of the men without respect for human rights, then men are really in trouble.

It was all right for folks back east to give reasons why trouble should be handled without violence. Folks who talk about no violence are always the ones who are first to call a policeman, and usually they are sure there's one handy.

The Daybreakers

The way to stay out of trouble was to avoid the places where trouble was.

When a difficulty develops, unless one can

help, it was far better to get away from the area and leave it to those whose business it was to handle such things.

Lonely on the Mountain

. . . the most serious trouble between men comes not so much from money, horses, or women, but from notions. A man takes a dislike to another man for no reason at all but that they rub each other wrong, and then something, a horse or a woman or a drink sets it off and they go shooting or cutting or walloping with sticks.

The Daybreakers

. . . I think a man takes trouble with him.

Galloway

Every man wishes to believe that when trouble appears he will stand up to it, yet no man knows it indeed before it happens.

Lando

A man can fight if he has to, but the worst thing he can do is to go looking for trouble. Of course he can make a fool of himself by assuming the other fellow wants peace, too, and this is a mistake sometimes made, for many Indians have nothing to gain except through war.

Chancy

When trouble showed, when I was faced with it, I just naturally stiffened my neck and went ahead. There was a streak of wildness in me, a streak of recklessness that I disliked. The cool way was the best way, that I knew, but at times I just naturally went hog-wild and started throwing lead or punches at whatever was in the way. It was going to get me killed some day.

Mustang Man

The more ill-prepared people are to face trouble, the more likely they are to revert to savagery against each other.

Bendigo Shafter

This was a hard land, and the rules were written plain in the way we lived. If you overstepped the rules you had bought yourself trouble.

The Lonely Men

. . . a man had best have no one to think of but himself if trouble comes.
Bendigo Shafter

A bad reputation can get a man in a lot of trouble, but once in a while it can be a help.
Ride the Dark Trail

All the enemies of whom I knew were far from here, yet any stranger was a potential enemy, and he was a wise traveler who was forever alert.
Jubal Sackett

Too often when trouble arises there is too much time wasted in trying to temporize, and it becomes too late for action.
Bendigo Shafter

It's like this. He's covered, see? The perfect crime. But no man who has committed a crime, a major crime, is ever sure he's safe. There is always a little doubt, a little fear. He may have overlooked something; somebody might recognize him.

That's where he's vulnerable. In his mind.

We can't find him, so we'll make him come to us!

The Hills of Homicide

Thievery . . . is a crime only for the very ignorant, in which only the most stupid would indulge. There is a crass vulgarity in theft, an indication that one lacks wit, and the penalties far outweigh the possible gain.

The Walking Drum

It is wrong to believe that such men suffer in the conscience for what they do . . . it is only regret at being caught that troubles them. And they never admit it was any fault of their own . . . it was always chance, bad luck. . . . The criminal does not regret his crime, he only regrets failure.

Lando

Men of violence only understand violence, most times.

The Daybreakers

Ange, when men carry guns they don't just talk about killing. When a man mentions killing, and has in his hands or on his person

144

the means to kill, then you have a right to believe he means to do what he says. I've helped bury a few men who tried to argue at times like that.

Sackett

A man who shoots when you don't call out doesn't have too many friends, but his enemies are surely all dead.

Treasure Mountain

There's an old adage that to win a street fight one had best land the first punch.

Bendigo Shafter

A man can lose sight of everything else when he's bent on revenge, and it ain't worth it.

Comstock Lode

The killing of a man was nothing of which to be proud. We lived in a hard time, and if men took guns in their hands to force others to their will, they had to expect to be killed. And they always were . . . sooner or later.

Bendigo Shafter

My pa always said you should never walk

into a man when he's set for punching. Better to go around him and work him out of balance.

The Sky-Liners

Another thing Pa had taught us boys was that anger is a killing thing: it kills the man who angers, for each rage leaves him less than he had been before—it takes something from him.

Mojave Crossing

He remembered only too well the words of the man long ago, who had told him revenge could steal a man's life until there was nothing left but emptiness.

Comstock Lode

Hate would destroy him who hated.

The Lonesome Gods

Hate clouds the mind. It is better to have no emotion when it is work. Do what needs to be done, and do it coolly.

Last of the Breed

146

A man who rides a violent road comes to only one end—up a dry creek somewhere, or on Boot Hill.

The Sky-Liners

. . . people have a greater tolerance for evil than for violence.

The Daybreakers

If a man or woman is inclined to murder or violence, owning a gun is not important. There are always a dozen things about with which a man can be killed.

To the Far Blue Mountains

. . . but a hand properly used can be as dangerous as a knife. . . . And a man is not lynched for what he does with his hands.

Lando

. . . anything could be a weapon, that men had been killing each other for a million years before a gun was invented, and if one did not have a gun, there was always something.

The Lonesome Gods

A political revolution always destroys more than it creates.

Last of the Breed

If ever you become a hero to the mob . . . remember this: Every man who cheers you carries in his belt the knife of an assassin.

The Walking Drum

. . . we boys learned to use guns mighty early, but we also learned to hold them in respect. When a man puts a gun on you, you've no cause to believe he won't use it.

Mustang Man

To have killed men is not a thing of which one can be proud. . . . A man uses a gun when necessary, and not too often, or carelessly.

Mojave Crossing

Just knowin' how to shoot is one thing, knowin' when to shoot is something else again, an' your pa has savvy.

The Lonesome Gods

. . . it is not necessary to have a gun or a

knife to kill. Everywhere are weapons! . . .
Any object that can be picked up can be a
weapon.

Comstock Lode

My blade cuts both ways, so be quick.

The Walking Drum

Any man can shoot a gun, and with practice
he can draw fast and shoot accurately, but
that makes no difference. What counts is
how you stand up when somebody is shooting back at you.

Sackett

Strange men they were, but I'd see their like
again, in lynch mobs and elsewhere. They
were men who knew what I did not—they
knew how to hate.

Lando

He had a notion to shoot, but when he saw
that big six in my hand he had another
notion that beat that first one all hollow.

Mojave Crossing

149

. . . a guilty man is very apt to suspect folks know more than they do. . . .

Bendigo Shafter

. . . they could part your hair with the first bullet and trim around your ears with the next two.

The Sky-Liners

Long ago I'd been taught that all guns were to be considered as loaded and were to be handled with care. . . .

The Lonesome Gods

When you take a hand in the gun game, you never know what the other man's holdin'.

Passin' Through

. . . pride and whiskey are a bad combination. . . .

The Daybreakers

Now a man expecting trouble had better not miss anything.

Treasure Mountain

. . . only a fool shot at what he could not identify.

Comstock Lode

He did not shoot hastily, yet he did fire rapidly, and there was a difference, for he seemed to make every shot count.

The Lonesome Gods

When a man uses a gun he'd better have a good reason, even if he does have a good lawyer.

Comstock Lode

A lot of people hear about violence but never come face to face with it, and they've no experience with men of violence. One thing I'd learned a long time back: you just can't waste time talking. If there's talking to do, do it afterwards.

Mustang Man

I prefer killing to being killed. One may talk of peace only with those who are peaceful. To talk of peace with him who holds a drawn sword is foolish unless one is unarmed, then one must talk very fast, indeed.

The Walking Drum

One thing I'd learned a long time back. When traveling in enemy country, never return by the same trail you used in going out . . . they may be laying for you.

The Sackett Brand

I believe in forgiving one's enemies, but keep your hand on your gun while you do it, mentally, at least. Because while you are forgiving him he may be studying ways to get at you.

Galloway

The terrorist lives for terror, not for the change he tells himself he wants. He masks his desire to kill and destroy behind the curtain of a cause. It is destruction he wants, not creation.

Last of the Breed

Beware of those who would use violence, too often it is the violence they want and neither truth nor freedom.

The Walking Drum

When a man begins a life of violence, or when he decides to live by taking something away from others, he just naturally points himself toward one end. He can't win—the odds are too much against him.

Mustang Man

There would be trouble enough, but man is born to trouble, and it is best to meet it when it comes and not lose sleep until it does.

The Daybreakers

Survival

How long a man lasts depends on how careful he is, and on the breaks of the game. Out here in this country a bullet or an arrow was only one way to go; there were many other ways—your horse could step in a prairie-dog hole when running; you could be gored by an outlaw steer, thrown by a horse, drowned in a river-crossing, caught in quicksand, or trampled in a stampede.

Chancy

I have found it is better to eat when one can, for one never knows when he will eat again.

Sackett's Land

Man had enemies, that was in the nature of things, but when it comes right down to it his battle to live is with that world out there, the cold, the rain, the wind—the heat, the

154

drought, and the sun-parched pools where water had been.

Treasure Mountain

Only two things a man really needs in this country to survive, a gun and a horse. . . . Come to think of it, though, there is something else.
Water.

Mojave Crossing

Many's the time I've suspected something when I was wrong; but there were other times I'd been right, and so I was still among the living.

The Sky-Liners

Sometimes the damned fool things a man does are the ones that save his bacon.

Mojave Crossing

A body shouldn't heed what might be. He's got to do with what is.

Treasure Mountain

There's few things a man can do that might not get him killed. It's a rough land, but a man is better off if he rides his trail knowing there may be trouble about. It simply won't do to get careless. . . .

The Sky-Liners

If they wish to survive in this new world, they must work.

The Lonesome Gods

. . . Trumpet among the elephants, crow among the cocks, bleat among the goats.

The Walking Drum

A man who travels with another is only half as watchful as when traveling alone, and often less than half, for a part of his attention is diverted by his companion.

Jubal Sackett

I could do with the comp'ny and the cookin', but a man listens better when he's alone, and he hears better.

Treasure Mountain

Watch out of the corners of your eyes. You pick up movement quicker that way.

The Lonesome Gods

In the wilderness attention to detail was the price of survival.

The Warrior's Path

I was pretty sure I'd come away from the Empty without being seen, but a man can get killed taking things for granted.

Ride the Dark Trail

I always try to have a little something extra to put on when out in cold weather. Main thing a man has to avoid is sweating. When he stops moving that sweat can freeze into an icy sheet inside the clothes.

Sackett

Folks like to camp close to streams for the sake of water, but crossing a big river was quite an operation, so they'd go into camp after they'd crossed over. That is, the smart ones would. Those who went into camp to cross over in the morning often found the water so high come morning they were stuck for several days.

Ride the Dark Trail

Always look. . . . A man in the forest, he

watches always and sees many places like this. He remembers, so if he comes that way again he knows where there is a camp.

Last of the Breed

Eat, boy, and do not stand on time. The food will stay with you and the memory of it where you go. My mam said always to take a cargo of memories, whatever else, for when all is lost the memories remain.

To the Far Blue Mountains

I liked not to sleep too warm but cool enough to sleep lightly so my ears can hear what moves about.

The Warrior's Path

[towns died of . . .]

Lack of attention, I think. Lack of love, lack of the will to take a stand, a willingness to let things be, to not be involved . . . a peace at any price policy, I think.

Bendigo Shafter

Some folks start scannin' afar off, and gradu-ally work closer and, closer to theirselves. I do it the other way because if somethin' is close, I want to know it.

The Lonesome Gods

Hunger, thirst, and cold—man's first enemies, and no doubt his last.

Treasure Mountain

It is a thing a man must forever guard, that he not twist an ankle badly or break a leg, for to be down and helpless is often to die.

The Warrior's Path

A man can wait out a storm if he doesn't exhaust himself first.

Bendigo Shafter

Knowledge might be power, but it was also the key to survival.

The Walking Drum

We who lived in the forest regularly ran or walked from place to place as did the Indians. It was by far the best way to cover distance where few horses and fewer roads were to be found.

Jubal Sackett

I also knew that although a horse was faster, a man could run a horse to death over a distance.

The Lonesome Gods

You've an appetite. . . . I hope your teeth are big enough!

To the Far Blue Mountains

A little warmth and a little food and he felt much better. Man needs so little . . . yet he begins wanting so much.

Last of the Breed

Exhaustion is the greatest danger in the cold, for the body then has no reserves with which to fight its battle to survive.

Bendigo Shafter

They had a man's hatred to drive them; I had my wish to survive.

The Lonesome Gods

Enemies can be an incentive to survive and become someone in spite of them. Enemies can keep you alert and aware.

The Lonesome Gods

It was a lesson taught by caution: to stop nowhere without finding a way out, a means of escape.

The Walking Drum

There's a saying in the mountains that if you harm a cricket his friends will come and eat your socks. A hard time they would have with me, not having socks or anything else.

Galloway

I'm anything it takes to get the coon. When there's mines, I work at minin', and when there's cows, that's my game. A man has to adjust.

Passin' Through

. . . Fool thing, looking into a fire. When you look away you're blind . . . and men have been killed thataway.

Mojave Crossing

. . . there's such a thing as reaction time. A man's got to realize what is happening, what has to be done, and he has to do it, all in the same moment.

The Sky-Liners

161

When one acts quickly, sometimes one acts too quickly.

Bendigo Shafter

A stick fighter never swings a wide blow— he thrusts or strikes with the end, and for the belly, the throat, or the eyes.

Lando

. . . if I was to survive I must understand this, that I must be tolerant even when others were intolerant, that I must be wary of man.

The Lonesome Gods

Wherever two cultures collide, the one with the most efficient way of living will survive.

Bendigo Shafter

If one would remain hidden . . . one must be obvious, not mysterious. Had I not told them who I was and who you were, they would have been curious, which leads to imaginings. . . . My identity is established, and we are no longer of interest.

The Walking Drum

162

Disappearing is one of the least easy things to do if a body has any recognizable way of living. We all set patterns, and if we break them somebody is sure to notice, although it may be somebody we don't even know.

Treasure Mountain

A man who lives on the rough side of things learns to trust to his instincts. The life he leads calls for a kind of alertness no man living a safe and regular life would need; his senses become sharper and they make him alive to things he can't always put into words.

Mustang Man

Oh, I took a drink now and again but had never been drunk in my life and never wanted to be. I always figured if I had my wits about me I could figure my way out of any corner I might get into. . . .

Passin' Through

My hand felt for a leaf, which was wet, and I put the wet fingers to my nose, for a wet nose smells better.

The Warrior's Path

Too often in emergencies had I seen people

who took the time to ask "Why" not live long enough to receive an answer.

The Warrior's Path

To exist is to adapt, and if one could not adapt, one died and made room for those who could.

Last of the Breed

To live was to struggle, and to keep our homes supplied with food and fuel was an unending task, allowing little time for considering things beyond the range of our daily lives. What we did not possess we had to make for ourselves or learn to do without, but the little I learned helped me to build a defense against the change that time would surely bring. . . .

Bendigo Shafter

A lot of what a man sees is sort of instinct, I guess. You notice how the shadows fall, and if there's a thicker shadow than should be, or a shadow where none had been before, you take care.

Passin' Through

Now in most places a man can live if he knows something of plants and animals, and if he will take time enough to think things out. It is a man's brain that . . . will let him survive, if he takes time to think.

Galloway

Death

To die for what one believes is all very well for those so inclined, but it has always seemed to me the most vain of solutions. There is no cause worth dying for that is not better served by living.

The Walking Drum

It was not in me to believe myself fated to die at any given time. Deep within me I knew, having seen many men die, that no man is immune to death at any time at all. During every moment, waking or sleeping, we are vulnerable. . . .

Mojave Crossing

If he be a man indeed, he must always go on, he must always endure. Death is an end to torture, to struggle, to suffering, but it is also an end to warmth, light, the beauty of a running horse, the smell of damp leaves, of gunpowder, the walk of a woman when she knows someone watches. . . .

Galloway

Death never spent time in my thoughts, for where a man is there is no death, and when death is there a man is gone, or the image of him.

Treasure Mountain

It is the measure of a man to die well.

Last of the Breed

When a man lives with the wilderness he comes to an acceptance of death as a part of living, he sees the leaves fall and rot away to build the soil for other trees and plants to be born.

Treasure Mountain

The man who is no longer on guard is one who invites death.

The Walking Drum

. . . death is a visitor who can call upon any man.

The Walking Drum

167

. . . the place a man leaves is in the hearts of those he leaves behind, and in his work, not upon a slab . . .

Sackett's Land

I do not expect to be remembered . . . only enjoyed.

The Walking Drum

He was a warrior, and for a warrior any day was a good day to die.

Last of the Breed

A man would be crazy to risk dying in a world where there was jasmine.

The Walking Drum

Every man is born with death in him. . . . It's only a matter of time.

Mojave Crossing

"You have saved my life," he said quietly.

"Wait. Perhaps I have only made you aware of death. We do not yet know what the night may bring."

The Walking Drum

When you don't see a body laid away, that person is never quite dead for you, just sort of gone away, or not around right then.

Treasure Mountain

I figure it's like the Plains Indians say—a happy hunting ground. Leastways, that's how I'd like it to be. A place with mountains, springs, running streams, and some green, grassy banks where a man can lie with his hat over his eyes and let the bees buzz.

Conagher

. . . the buzzard has only to wait. In the end, we all come to him or his like.

The Lonesome Gods

When I die, remember that what you knew of me is with you always. What is buried is only the shell of what was. Do not regret the shell, but remember the man. Remember the father.

Last of the Breed

War and Fighting

No matter how many times you get knocked down you got to keep gettin' up until the other man quits.

Treasure Mountain

But fighting is like playing poker. You have to pay to learn, and you only learn with the cards in hand and money on the table.

Lonely on the Mountain

Thing about fightin' with folks unused to fightin' is that a body should give them time. They get eager to get on with it and haven't the patience to set and wait.

Treasure Mountain

My father had always told me the way to win was to attack. No matter how outnumbered, there was always a good way to attack.

Sackett's Land

170

In such fighting there is no sportsmanship, for it is no game but is in deadly earnest, and men fight to win.

Lando

Nobody ever won a fight by setting back and waiting, at least, not in my circumstances. In any case, my only way of fighting was to attack, and I believe in it, anyway.

Treasure Mountain

What I mean is, I had a bull by the tail and I was safe as long as I hung on; but I had to let go sometime, and it was better to pick my own time than to wait until he got impatient.

Mojave Crossing

. . . but a body can't always have things the way he figures, and I was doing my figuring without remembering the horse I was on.

Chancy

Now, there's a thing about fighting when the chips are down. You get a man going, you don't let up on him. He's apt to come back and beat your ears down.

The Sky-Liners

171

. . . fightin's something you do when you've tried everything else.

The Lonesome Gods

Just because a man can shoot, it doesn't turn him into a fightin' man.

Lonely on the Mountain

Fighting is a craft, and it must be learned and practiced. Until you know how to fight with your head as well as with heart and muscle, you are no fighting man.

Lando

If an enemy can be pushed into moving in haste, he may be pushed into mistakes and indiscretions.

The Walking Drum

So much of any fight depends on the terrain and how a body uses it.

The Sky-Liners

My father, a skilled fighting man, always told me to notice the position of a man's feet, for if a man can be taken off-balance he can be beaten. There is a limit to how far a man can reach without shifting his feet.

The Walking Drum

A man can always fight . . . but sometimes there are other ways.

The Lonesome Gods

No matter what they'd done or tried to do I was still alive. I knew what was happening to me and a man who can feel is a man who can fight.

Ride the Dark Trail

You see, Ox, you've always been big, you've always been strong, you've always been able to either frighten or out-muscle anybody whose trail you crossed. So the truth is, you've never really had to learn to fight.

Lonely on the Mountain

Once in a while a man has to fight . . . but you avoid it if you can. Fightin' attracts attention, and that's the last thing you need.

The Lonesome Gods

One fights one's battles alone, not asking mercy nor expecting help.

To the Far Blue Mountains

To survive at all, I must fight only to win.
The Walking Drum

There are a lot of women, a lot of wine and whiskey down that road, and if you stay here, there's only a mouthful of blood, teeth, and the dirt you'll bite into while dying.
The Lonesome Gods

Cruelty was a rare thing in the war. Fireside folks who talk about war and read about it, they figure it's cruel more often than not, but it simply isn't so. . . .

You kill in war because it is your job, and because you want to survive, and not because of any desire to kill.
Mojave Crossing

My father was a soldier and he always told me a good soldier never stood when he could sit, never sat when he could lie down, and ate whenever there was food.
Sackett's Land

. . . carry the sword, charge the pistols, and sleep not too well.
Sackett's Land

. . . I learned then that many a victory is easier won with words than a sword—and the results are better.

The Walking Drum

Yet when a man walks out with weapons his life is suspended like dew upon a spider's web. . . .

Jubal Sackett

The smell of fight was in my nostrils also, for I was young, and youth expects to live forever. Youth has not yet discovered that death recognizes no age limits.

The Walking Drum

Many men avoid battle not from cowardice but from fear of cowardice, fear that when the moment of truth comes they will not have the courage to face up to it.

Treasure Mountain

Sometimes a show of force can prevent trouble.

Comstock Lode

The art of war can be learned. . . . But after

the principles are learned the rest is ingenuity, the gift that goes beyond learning, or the instinct born of understanding.

Sackett's Land

It is one thing to be fierce in battle, but it is important, also, to be wise in council.

Conagher

The army can destroy, the furrow can feed.

The Lonesome Gods

Like a lot of others he was ready to hurt or kill, but not to be hurt or killed.

Treasure Mountain

Seems to me a man has trouble enough in this world without borrowing more with careless words.

Mojave Crossing

. . . with a sword a man might win a kingdom, might hold that kingdom against all who came—and might also lose his head for trying.

Sackett's Land

A man wants peace in a country he has to go straight to the heart of things.

The Daybreakers

He'd used a gun enough to know that you don't just shoot somebody and they fall down. If a man is mad and coming at you, you have to get him right through the heart, right through the brain, or on a big bone to stop him. On the other hand, a shot that's unexpected can drop a man in his tracks. . . .

Mustang Man

Six to one might seem long odds but if a man has nerve enough and if he thinks in terms of combat, the advantage is often against sheer numbers. Sheer numbers rob a man of something and he begins to depend . . . and in a fighting matter no man should depend. He should do what has to be done himself.

The Daybreakers

There was a Texas Ranger one time who said that there's no stopping a man who knows he's in the right and keeps a-coming.

Sackett

. . . enemies can make one strong.

The Lonesome Gods

One thing . . . never underestimate an enemy!

Last of the Breed

Never let an enemy get set. . . . Attack, worry, keep him off balance. Never let him move from a secure position or give him time to move his pieces on the chessboard.

The Warrior's Path

We were sentimental men, but that was our secret, for an enemy who knows your feelings is an enemy who has a hold on you. Not all poker is played over a card table.

The Lonely Men

You fool around with the band wagon, son . . . and you're liable to get hit with the horn.

Conagher

A man needs enemies to keep him wary and strong. . . .

Conagher

If one plans to measure blows with a stranger, one had best judge the length of his arm.

The Walking Drum

This is our fight. They opened the ball, now we're going to play the tune and they'll dance to our music.

The Sky-Liners

Sometimes men are born who just can't abide one another from the time they meet . . . don't make no rhyme nor reason, but it's so. . . .

Tom's gone killer. . . . It infects some men like rabies, and they keep on killing until somebody kills them.

The Daybreakers

. . . for today he who rides before an army may tomorrow lie in its dust.

The Walking Drum

. . . there are times to fight and times to run and the wise man is one who can choose the right time for each.

The Daybreakers

. . . a wise man fights to win, but he is twice a fool who has no plan for possible defeat.

The Walking Drum

All his life there had been a battle, and all his life he had worked. He would go down working, go down fighting, go out trying as he had always done. Had he known how, he would have quit, but life had taught him everything but that.

Comstock Lode

Yondering and Dreaming

Men move across the face of the world like tides upon the sea, and when they have gone, others will come; and the weak would pass and the strong would live, for that was the way it was, and the way it would be.

For a little while men might change that, but in the last analysis men would not decide. It would be the wind, the rain, the tortured earth, and the looming mountains, it would be drought and hunger, it would be cold and desolation. For it is these elements that decide, and no man can build a wall strong enough to keep them out forever.

Bendigo Shafter

Knowledge is awareness, and to it there are many paths, not all of them paved with logic. But sometimes one is guided through the maze by intuition. One is led by something felt on the wind, something seen in the stars, something that calls from the wastelands to the spirit.

The Lonesome Gods

There is always hope for a man who can dream, and even for one who can boast, for when the two are together they try to bring both to reality.

Sackett's Land

For I wanted a life wider and deeper than my own Breton shores could offer. To make my way in a larger world, to see more, to learn more, to be more. This was my dream.

The Walking Drum

Forever the dream is in the mind, realization in the hands.

To the Far Blue Mountains

I know nothing of these stories. I only know what I have said, that where men can go, they will go, and what is so hard about crossing a sea? It is sailing along shore that is dangerous, and men had sailed from Egypt to Crete and even to the western ocean shores of Spain in the time of Solomon, which is a farther distance than from Iceland to America.

To the Far Blue Mountains

One who returns to a place sees it with new eyes. Although the place may not have changed, the viewer inevitably has. For the first time things invisible before become suddenly visible.

Bendigo Shafter

Seems to me folks waste a sight of time crossing bridges before they get to them. They clutter their minds with odds and ends that interfere with clear thinking.

Treasure Mountain

Yet the spirit of inquiry was alive here, and where it has a free existence, ignorance cannot last.

The Walking Drum

Remember this . . . our world is one where the impossible occurs every day, and what we often call supernatural is simply the misunderstood.

The Lonesome Gods

183

The mind gathers its grain in all fields, storing it against a time of need, then suddenly it bursts into awareness, which men call inspiration or second sight or a gift.

The Walking Drum

Men do not like puzzles, Barnabas. They prefer categories. It is far easier to slip a piece of information into a known slot than to puzzle over the unknown.

To the Far Blue Mountains

There's no way I know of that a body can foresee the future, but sometimes he can read it pretty well if he knows the way folks think.

Mustang Man

My future is one I must make myself. . . .

Sackett's Land

It is man's nature, Itchakomi, to wonder, and thank all the gods for it. It is through wonder that we come to know.

Jubal Sackett

Most of all I needed what all men need, a

destination. I wanted to become something, for in the last analysis it is not what people think of a man but what he thinks of himself.

Bendigo Shafter

"It is not enough to *do*, one must also *become*. I wish to be wiser, stronger, better. This—" I held out my hands—"this thing that is me is incomplete. It is only the raw material with which I have to work. I want to make it better than I received it."

Jubal Sackett

For land beyond the mountains is ever a dream and a challenge, and each generation needs that, that dream of some far-off place to go.

To the Far Blue Mountains

And when the frontiers of our own land are gone, when we have drawn them all into an ordered world, then we must seek other frontiers, the frontiers of the mind beyond which men have not gone, the frontiers that lie out beyond the stars, the frontiers that lie within

185

our own selves, that hold us back from what we would do, what we would achieve.

Bendigo Shafter

There are always the shores beyond, for this have the gods given to men: that we shall always have those farther shores, always a dream to follow, always a sea for questing. . . . Only in seeking is man important, seeking for answers, and in the shadow he leaves upon the land.

The Walking Drum

I suspect each of us rode toward a different shrine, the same only in name. For the destination men name is only the destination of surface: For each there is another, a different destination.

Bendigo Shafter

He might never really do what he said, but at least he had it in mind. He had somewhere to go.

Comstock Lode

The saddle is a place for dreaming when there's hours of trail ahead, or when night-

186

herding. And it came over me that to be rich was not enough. A man must win respect, and not the kind that can be bought with money or won with a gun. My pa always taught me that a man should strive to become somebody.

Chancy

He always thought better while working, walking, or riding. Somehow physical activity was conducive to thinking, at least if the activity called for no particular attention.

Comstock Lode

Some of the mountain men were finely educated, some were not, but all were extremely practical men whose minds were beautifully tuned. They could not be dull, for to let their wits dull was to invite death.

The Lonesome Gods

The first goal need not be the final one, for a sailing ship sails first by one wind, then another. The point is that it is always going somewhere, proceeding toward a final destination.

The Walking Drum

Sometimes we have the dream but we are not ourselves ready for the dream. We have to grow to meet it.

Bendigo Shafter

The way I saw it unless a man knows where he's going he isn't going anywhere at all. . . .

Time has a way of running out from under a man. Looked like a man would never amount to much without book learning and every day folks were talking of what they had read, of what was happening, but none of it made any sense to me who had to learn by listening. When a man learns by listening he is never sure whether he is getting the straight of things or not.

The Daybreakers

Going on would have been simple, for travel is an escape, and as long as our wagons moved our decisions could be postponed. When one moves, one is locked in the treadmill of travel, and all decisions must await a destination.

Bendigo Shafter

He who would see a far land must carry the

far land in his heart. The heat, dust, and struggle are a part of it; these were what made the beauties worth having.

The Walking Drum

I do not know, but I think it is something buried within us, something that makes us long for the far places.

Jubal Sackett

Your father would tell me we will never know how much of the world was explored. The sea was often difficult to cross, but it was never impossible, and it has been crossed again and again by craft of every size and material.

The Lonesome Gods

It goes to show you. People don't wear out, they give up. And as far as trails go, there's always an open trail for the mind if you keep the doors open and give it a chance.

Bendigo Shafter

Speak little, listen much. In Córdoba there is beauty and there is wisdom, but there is blood, also.

The Walking Drum

Lead on, lead on! A true philosopher will never refuse a lass, a glass, or an hour of conversation!

The Walking Drum

. . . perhaps he is a poet whose dreams are too large for his words.

The Lonesome Gods

When men have gone down the longest rivers, climbed the highest mountains, and crossed the greatest deserts there will still be the stars. . . .

Who knows if this is true or not? But do you think men will be content to wonder? Someday they will find a way to the stars and an answer to their questions.

Jubal Sackett

The publishers hope that this
Large Print Book has brought
you pleasurable reading.
Each title is designed to make
the text as easy to see as possible.
G.K. Hall Large Print Books
are available from your library and
your local bookstore. Or, you can
receive information by mail on
upcoming and current Large Print Books
and order directly from the publishers.
Just send your name and address to:

G.K. Hall & Co.
70 Lincoln Street
Boston, Mass. 02111

or call, toll-free:

1-800-343-2806

A note on the text
Large print edition designed by
Bernadette Montalvo.
Composed in 18 pt Plantin
on a Xyvision 300/Linotron 202N
by Michael Kelley
of G.K. Hall & Co.